STUDY GUIDE TO ACCOMPANY

CHILDREN

DEVELOPMENT AND SOCIAL ISSUES

Betty Ann Ward and Kathryn T. Young
in collaboration with
Edward F. Zigler and Matia Finn-Stevenson
all of Yale University

D. C. HEATH AND COMPANY
Lexington, Massachusetts   Toronto

PREFACE

One of the most difficult tasks students face is discovering how to use a finite number of waking hours to satisfy a rapidly multiplying number of goals and demands. Some solve this dilemma by radically reducing the amount of time they spend sleeping. We think there is a better answer. Thus, the major purpose of the *Study Guide to Accompany Children: Development and Social Issues* is to provide you with tools, such as study goals, chapter reviews, lists of key terms, and practice questions, that will help you make the most efficient use of your study time. In the following section, "Using this Study Guide," we have offered some advice on how to employ these tools to best advantage. We realize however, that each student will use the guide a bit differently, and we have designed it to assist either a quick, pre-test review or a more systematic, long-term study plan.

USING THIS STUDY GUIDE

Each chapter in this study guide corresponds to a chapter in *Children: Development and Social Issues* and is composed of four elements:

1. *Study Goals:* A list of things you should know after studying the chapter

2. *Reviewing the Chapter:* A review of the chapter's content

3. *Significant Concepts, People, and Topics:* A list of words and concepts you should be able to explain

4. *Self-Check Questions:* A short set of multiple choice questions to permit you to assess the need for further study

The goals of each study guide chapter are to tell you what you need to know before taking an exam, to provide you with a structure that will assist your review, to increase your confidence in approaching either a multiple choice or an essay test, and to allow you to check your knowledge.

One way to make effective use of this guide is to adhere to the following study plan. Before reading each section of the textbook chapter, glance through the chapter outline and the study goals for that section. *After* reading, look over the chapter review for the section and attempt to meet the study goals. Before moving to the next section of the chapter in the textbook, go back and find responses for any study goals you cannot meet. Repeat this process for each section of the chapter until you have met all study goals. Next, turn to the list of terms, concepts, and people and look up in the chapter or glossary any whose meaning or significance you do not recognize from having read the chapter. Finally, depending on the amount of time left before your exam, reread the chapter itself or the chapter review and check your readiness by quickly going over the study goals and terms, concentrating on those with which you've had difficulty. You will find that the most effective way to make use of the self-check items is not to look at them until you feel truly prepared for a test. At that point, you should try to complete them without the assistance of the book. Your score on the self-check quiz will give you an idea of your readiness and will also indicate specific areas that may need further attention. If you miss several questions on the self-check, you will probably want to review the chapter again before taking your exam.

This is one way to use this guide. There are other effective ways to use it, however, and the method you adopt will depend on the time you have available for study, your habits, and a variety of other factors. Whatever pattern of use you choose, you will benefit most by spreading your reviews over as long a period as possible. It is axiomatic in educational psychology that spaced learning trials result in better retention than massed learning trials. In other words, reviewing the material for an hour per day over seven consecutive days will probably lead to a better test score than spending seven hours on the material the day before the test.

This preface is devoted to suggesting ways to use this study guide, but you should also know how it is best *not* to use it. With the time pressures all college students face, it is tempting to substitute reading chapter reviews for reading the chapters themselves. However, these are *reviews,* not summaries, and are intended to be used to refresh your memory once you've read the chapter in the textbook. They are necessarily brief and they can neither encompass all the material presented in a chapter nor can they devote space to defining terms already explained in the textbook. Consequently, the chapter review may appear somewhat dense or cryptic until you have read the corresponding portion of the textbook. Good luck in your study of child development!

ACKNOWLEDGEMENTS

Few large projects are completed without help, and the writers of this guide were assisted by several people whose contributions should be acknowledged. We would like to thank our collaborators, Edward F. Zigler and Matia Finn-Stevenson, for their generous assistance. Their cooperation and valuable contributions have ensured that the text and the study materials are well-integrated. We would also like to acknowledge John Servideo and Jim Miller of D. C. Heath and Company for their efficient administration and considerable patience. Away from the office, the supportiveness of Juanita, Craig, and Winona Ward and Jerry, Jessica, and Nicole Young made it considerably easier to complete this project and continues to be deeply appreciated.

CONTENTS

INTRODUCTION

THE STUDY OF CHILD DEVELOPMENT

STUDY GOALS

After reading and studying the Introduction, you should be able to:

1. Describe the goals of child development research and name several reasons for studying children.

2. Describe the types of activities through which developmental psychologists answer questions about children.

3. Identify the major figures in the history of child and adolescent psychology (Locke, Rousseau, Darwin, Hall, and Gesell) by describing their most important beliefs and contributions.

4. Identify the major figures in the testing movement (Binet, Simon, and Terman) and their accomplishments.

5. Define and discuss the nature-nurture controversy, describing both Locke's and Rousseau's beliefs regarding the nature of the child and human development.

6. Identify the attributes that define a theory.

7. Define and contrast epigenetic and environmental theories.

8. Match major theorists (Piaget, Werner, Freud, Erikson, Skinner, Pavlov, and Bandura) with their theoretical perspectives and contributions to developmental psychology.

9. Identify the differences and similarities among psychosocial, psychoanalytic, cognitive-developmental, and learning theories.

10. List the major criticisms that have been directed at psychoanalytic theory.

11. Describe the cross-cultural, genetic, comparative, ethological, and ecological approaches to child development research.

12. Identify the ways in which conclusions derived from personal experience are different from those derived from research.

1

13. Differentiate between applied and basic research and contrast descriptive and manipulative research.

14. Describe normative, observational, experimental, and correlational methods.

15. Distinguish a field experiment from a natural experiment.

16. Distinguish independent, dependent, and extraneous variables in the context of an experiment; recognize when an experiment is confounded and know the conditions that must be satisfied for an experiment to retain internal validity.

17. Understand the meaning of positive and negative correlations and know what conclusions can reasonably be drawn from correlational evidence.

18. Compare and contrast the longitudinal, cross-sectional, and retrospective research strategies. List the advantages and disadvantages of each strategy.

19. Discuss the ethical problems posed by conducting research with young children and describe the steps that a researcher must take to ensure ethical treatment of subjects.

20. Suggest some precautions that should be observed in applying the results of research to real-life problems.

REVIEWING THE CHAPTER

I. Why should we study children?
   (pp. 3–5; study goals 1 and 2)

   Knowledge of children's perceptions, feelings, thoughts, and interactions helps us to understand what to expect from children of different ages, assess the social trends that affect their lives, and may increase our understanding of development itself, which continues throughout life. Moreover, philosophers once argued that child study could further our understanding of the nature of man.

   The goal of child development research today is to understand the process of development by studying the changes that occur in children as they mature. This involves devising scientific methods for studying children, compiling information about children of different ages and backgrounds, and developing theories to explain children's behavior and developmental changes. Answering broad questions about child development requires synthesizing the results of many studies and observing children in both laboratory and natural contexts.

II. What is the history of developmental psychology?
   (pp. 5–13; study goals 3–5)

   John Locke, a 17th century English philosopher, argued that the young child's mind was like a blank slate on which experience would write. A century later, Jean-Jacques Rousseau described the child as a "noble savage," who possessed an intuitive sense of right and wrong. According to Rousseau, parents needed only to allow the child to explore the world around him rather than to provide a carefully controlled environment, as Locke advised. These different views led to the nature-nurture controversy, the debate over whether traits are endowed or wholly shaped by experience.

Charles Darwin promoted a scientific rather than a philosophic approach to child study in the 19th century. This began with baby biographies and other forms of careful observation. At the turn of the 20th century, G. Stanley Hall founded child and adolescent psychology by employing questionnaires to gather data from large groups of subjects, which could be used to test generalizations about development.

In France, Binet and Simon, the founders of the testing movement, developed the IQ test as an objective means of distinguishing normal from subnormal children. Defining the intelligence quotient (IQ) as the ratio of mental age to chronological age multiplied by 100, Binet and Simon validated their test by demonstrating that children with high IQs tended to perform better in school than those with lower IQs. Lewis Terman expanded upon Binet and Simon's work and extended it to America with the publication of the Stanford-Binet.

Arnold Gesell, one of Hall's students, developed standards for development in motor, visual, linguistic, and social behavior by photographing the development and behavior of full-term, pre-term, and impaired infants. He noted orderly stages of development that formed a universal and invariant sequence and he advanced a theory of maturational readiness. By the 1930s, child development was established as a discipline and began to move from data gathering to theory testing.

III. What is the role of theories of child development?
(pp. 13–25; study goals 6–10)

A theory is a way of organizing data to permit an understanding of a phenomenon and to provide direction for future research. A theory must be both testable and capable of generating hypotheses, though it may be either small or large in scope. A theory's usefulness is determined not by its accuracy, but by its ability to identify productive directions for research.

Current theories in child development are of two types: epigenetic theories (psychoanalytic, psychosocial, and cognitive-developmental) and environmental, or learning, theories. Freud's psychoanalytic account of development, Erikson's psychosocial theory, Werner's and Piaget's cognitive-developmental theories, and different types of learning theories are described on pages 15 to 25.

IV. How do adherents of different theories approach the study of child development?
(pp. 25–30; study goal 11)

The assumptions and characteristics of cross-cultural, genetic, comparative, ethological, and ecological approaches to child study and developmental questions are briefly described on pages 26 to 30.

V. How is child development research conducted?
   (pp. 31–42; study goals 12–20)

Research evidence, unlike personal experience, is derived from the study of representative samples of individuals using clearly described methods to form generalizable conclusions. Particular research efforts are often described by placing them along the applied/basic continuum or characterizing their methods as either descriptive or manipulative.

Methods used in research on child development include (1) the *normative method,* which documents when and in what sequence behaviors appear; (2) the *observational method,* which uses reliable and valid recordings of observed behavior to test hypotheses; (3) the *experimental method,* which manipulates independent variables and measures their effect on dependent variables while controlling extraneous variables to retain internal validity; and (4) the *correlational method,* which uses a statistic called a correlation to assess whether variables are positively or negatively related.

Longitudinal, cross-sectional, and retrospective research strategies are differentiated by *when* and *from whom* data is collected. The *longitudinal approach* entails repeatedly collecting data from the same group of subjects and comparing the data collected at Time 1 with the data collected from the *same* subjects at Time 2. This strategy allows researchers to investigate the stability or instability of behavior and the long-term effects of environmental factors. However, it is expensive, time-consuming, and plagued by unrepresentative samples, subject attrition, repeat-testing effects, and historical events that complicate the interpretation of results. The *cross-sectional approach* involves collecting data at only one point in time from groups of subjects at different age levels. This strategy is less time-consuming, but can be complicated by cohort effects. *Retrospective research* uses questionnaires or structured interviews to attempt to link an individual's current attitudes, characteristics, or behaviors with selected aspects of his or her earlier life.

There are many ethical questions to be faced in planning research and applying our knowledge. Independent review of research plans and adherence to ethical guidelines are required by law. In applying research results, we must remember that behavior has multiple causes and that there are wide individual differences among children.

SIGNIFICANT CONCEPTS, PEOPLE, AND TOPICS

You should become familiar with and be able to explain the following concepts, people, and topics. Most of the terms are highlighted in the margins of the text and some are also defined in the glossary at the end of the text. You should be able to associate each person named with his or her major accomplishments, theoretical orientation, or philosophical beliefs.

John Locke   *Jean-Jacques Rousseau*
Charles Darwin   *G. Stanley Hall*
Binet and Simon   *Lewis Terman*
Arnold Gesell   *Sigmund Freud*

Erik Erikson
Heinz Werner
Ivan Pavlov
Albert Bandura
baby biography
testability
epigenetic theories
psychoanalytic theory
ego
oral zone
genital period
positive fixation
psychosocial theory
cognition
cognitive structures
hierarchic integration
organizational stability
classical conditioning
behavior modifiers
genetic approach
ethological approach
species-typical behaviors
applied research
descriptive research
normative method
ecological validity
validity
generalizability
random assignment
dependent variables
confounded experiment
natural experiment
positive relationships
statistical significance
subject attrition
historical events
combined cross-sectional and longitu-
    dinal approach
case history

Jean Piaget
John B. Watson
B. F. Skinner
nature-nurture controversy
intelligence quotient (IQ)
hypothesis
environmental theories
id
superego
phallic zone
negative fixation
anal retentive
cognitive-developmental theory
epistemology
orthogenetic principle
adaptive change
learning theory
operant conditioning
cross-cultural approach
comparative approach
imprinting
ecological approach
basic research
manipulative research
observational method
reliability
representativeness
experimental method
independent variables
extraneous variables
field experiment
correlational method
negative relationships
longitudinal research
repeat testing
cross-sectional research
retrospective research
ethical standards

5

SELF-CHECK

Choose the response that best answers the question or completes the statement.

_____ 1. Which of the following individuals is most closely associated with first encouraging a *scientific* approach to child study?
  a. John Locke
  b. Jean-Jacques Rousseau
  c. Charles Darwin
  d. Jean Piaget

_____ 2. The comparative approach to child study refers to
  a. examining differences in behavior among different age groups.
  b. examining an aspect of human behavior in relation to similar behaviors in other species.
  c. a & b
  d. none of the above

_____ 3. A researcher conducts a study in which she examines the relationship between the amount of time children spend looking at a television program and their scores on a test of the program's content. She finds a correlation between looking time and test scores of 0.75. Which of the following conclusions can she draw from her finding?
  a. Looking time is only weakly related to memory for the program's content.
  b. As attention to the program increases, memory for the program's content decreases.
  c. Attention to the program causes increased memory for the program's content.
  d. Looking time and test scores are positively related.

_____ 4. Which of the following is *not* a disadvantage of longitudinal research?
  a. Subject attrition—some subjects drop out of the study.
  b. Subjects are unwilling to participate in a long study and those who do may not be representative of the larger population.
  c. Subjects' test scores may improve because they have become "test-wise" with repeated testings rather than because the abilities measured by the tests have really changed.
  d. Age differences in behaviors may be attributable to cohort effects rather than to real change with age.

_____ 5. Arnold Gesell photographed the development and behavior of many normal and abnormal children of different ages to arrive at standards, or benchmarks, for different types of developmental achievements. This is an example of
  a. descriptive research.
  b. manipulative research.
  c. the normative method.
  d. a & c

_____ 6. Which pair of people represents the most opposite views on the nature-nurture controversy?

a. Jean Piaget and Charles Darwin
b. Jean-Jacques Rousseau and John Locke
c. Jean-Jacques Rousseau and Charles Darwin
d. John Locke and Jean Piaget

_____ 7. Freud's and Erikson's accounts of development are similar because
a. they both focus on the individual's need to resolve conflicts.
b. they both emphasize emotional development throughout the lifespan.
c. in both theories, maladjustment is attributed to unsuccessful resolution of a conflict.
d. a & c

_____ 8. Conclusions derived from our personal observations and experiences with children cannot be generalized because
a. each of us defines behaviors differently.
b. the way we arrived at our conclusions is not well defined or open to inspection.
c. we may know an unrepresentative set of children.
d. all of the above

_____ 9. A psychologist wants to determine how the availability of toys affects children's social interaction. He finds an after-school program in which 40 children have been randomly assigned to one of two classrooms. Classroom 1 is supervised by Mr. Adams and Classroom 2 is supervised by Mr. Bunsen. The psychologist introduces 20 toys into Classroom 1, but only 10 toys are placed in Classroom 2. He and his assistant observe much more cooperative behavior in Classroom 2, but later the psychologist learns that Mr. Bunsen is a more strict and controlling classroom supervisor than Mr. Adams. In this example, classroom supervisor is
a. a dependent variable.
b. an independent variable.
c. an extraneous variable.
d. none of the above

_____ 10. Normally, someone who plans to conduct research with young children must
a. have his or her research plans approved by an institutional review board.
b. inform the child and his or her parents as fully as possible and obtain the parents' consent.
c. a & b
d. none of the above

Answers to Self-Check Questions

1. c	**6.** b
2. b	**7.** d
3. d	**8.** d
4. d	**9.** c
5. d	**10.** c

NEW DIRECTIONS IN CHILD DEVELOPMENT:
A SOCIAL ISSUES APPROACH

STUDY GOALS

After reading and studying Chapter 1, you should be able to:

1. Identify two major goals of research.

2. List the advantages, for researchers in the field of child development, of becoming involved in the development, evaluation, or implementation of social programs or policies.

3. Describe childhood social indicators, list the ways they can be of use to us, and name several examples of this type of indicator.

4. Describe the types of activities in which advocates engage.

5. Explain how children's lives are affected by society's conception of childhood.

6. Summarize the changes, since 1700, in ideas about children and in the conditions under which children have lived.

7. Describe our current conception of childhood and the direction in which it appears to be changing.

8. Describe how the demographic configuration of American society has changed in recent years and indicate which segments of our population are growing, which segments are shrinking, and the factors that have been suggested to explain these trends.

9. Explain the problems these demographic changes may pose for members of the next generation by referring to the new family policy of the People's Republic of China and the problems it has encountered.

10. Characterize today's American families, describe the various types of family forms; and list the challenges confronted by adults and children in single-parent, traditional, divorced, two-worker, and step-families.

11. Name the factors that are associated with the coping ability of children from divorced families.

12. List the positive and negative influences of television on family interaction.

13. Contrast the characteristics of television with those of print media, and discuss how these differences in the media affect their influence on consumers.

14. Summarize the arguments used to justify the limitation or regulation of television advertising directed at children.

15. Discuss the link between aggressive behavior and television viewing and describe the evidence used to support this association.

16. Describe the goals and characteristics of family support programs.

17. Discuss the role of government in assisting families and explain the historical importance of the Social Security Act of 1935.

18. List several ways in which child development experts and child advocates may assist government, business, and industry to facilitate family life.

REVIEWING THE CHAPTER

I. How can research affect social problems and vice versa?
(p. 46; study goals 1 and 2)

Acceptance of the notion that solving social problems is an appropriate goal for research has caused many researchers to become involved in the development or evaluation of social programs and policies. In the 1960s, researchers' involvement in the implementation of social programs helped them to refine their research methodologies, increase their understanding of children and the factors that impinge on their development, and develop natural laboratories, such as Head Start, that facilitate child study.

II. What are childhood social indicators?
(pp. 46–48; study goals 3 and 4)

Childhood social indicators measure the changes or constancies in the conditions of children's lives and the health, achievement, behavior, and well-being of children themselves. They help parents, professionals, and child advocates to understand the influence of social changes on the development of children, to devise ways to help children, and to bring social issues affecting children to the attention of policymakers.

III. How have ideas about children changed over time?
(pp. 48–54; study goals 5–7)

Our ideas about the nature of the child and our perception of the meaning and place of childhood in the social order have varied with time. These ideas and perceptions influence the way children are treated, the conditions under which they live, the concerns we have for them, and the policies we create for their

9

benefit. Our current conception of childhood as a special period of the life cycle is peculiar to the technological societies of this century.

In the years following 1700, when European documentation improved, records indicate that children were born in great numbers, but that infant and childhood mortality, abandonment, and neglect were so high that there appears to have been no special emotional attachment to children. Perhaps this was because the chances for children's survival were so slim. In the 1800s, middle-class childhood was characterized by subjection to firm discipline intended to encourage moral salvation, while poor children were often pushed into the work force. However, by the early 1900s, children were recognized as needing education and protection, which heralded the introduction of child labor laws and compulsory schooling. In the years of affluence following World War II, when most American families were able to live on a single income, our society may have reached a peak of child-centeredness. Since 1970, evidence has accumulated that society is moving away from its focus on children and families.

IV. What is it like to grow up in the 1980s?
(pp. 54–74; study goals 8–15)

A. How has our population changed in recent years?
(pp. 54–60; study goals 8 and 9)

The 1980s have been characterized by technological changes, economic problems, a revolution in the way men and women perceive their roles in work and family life, and a plethora of demographic changes. The latter have resulted in an aging population; the birth rate has declined due partly to later marriage and childbearing, the ranks of young adults are increasing as the post-war baby boom matures, and the numbers of older individuals are increasing as medical advances lengthen the lifespan. These demographic changes may mean that children born in the years just ahead will be faced not only with ensuring the well-being of their own progeny, but also with providing assistance to larger and larger numbers of older individuals. In addition, they will compete for career advancement with the many members of the baby-boom generation, who will not reach retirement until the turn of the century. The West may learn a great deal about the effects of such demographic changes by monitoring the impact of the policy adopted by the People's Republic of China, whose systematic preference for single-child families can be viewed as a natural experiment in demographic change.

B. How have families changed?
(pp. 60–70; study goals 10 and 11)

Increases in divorce, single-parenthood, and mothers' participation in the work force have led to changes in family life and family characteristics. Among these changes is an increase in the formation of step-families (also called blended families, reconstituted families, or new extended families), which has contributed to a new variety of family forms, each with its own strengths and weaknesses.

One fifth of all children and half of all black children live in *single-parent families*. Over half of the minors who live in single-parent families live below the poverty level, and it is to poverty and to the problems associated with divorce that the difficulties of children from this family form are attributed. Stress caused by task-overload is also a frequent problem for single parents.

Divorce is a major contributor to the rising number of single-parent families. Usually within a year or two after divorce, family members have managed to adjust to the restructuring of the family, loss of a family member, and new ways of family functioning. The degree to which children are able to cope with these changes has been associated with age, the presence of siblings, the psychological status of the custodial parent, the availability and involvement of the non-custodial parent, birth order, and sex. Following divorce, parents often experience stresses which may contribute to depression, problems in the care and behavioral management of children, or failure to recognize children's painful divorce experiences and a tendency to confide in children on complex matters. Some parents may even use legal battles over child custody to vent rage against a former spouse.

In making a transition from a single-parent family to a *step-family,* children must adjust to a new family structure, new family members, and the values and discipline practices of two different homes. Ten percent of children under 18 currently live in this family form.

Recently, increased maternal employment has enlarged the number of *dual-income families.* There is no body of research to indicate that women's working outside the home harms children. Maternal employment can help families keep pace with inflation or stay out of poverty, increase some women's happiness and satisfaction, enable children to play a useful role in family life, and provide children with new perceptions of male and female roles in society. However, the inadequate supply of day care in the United States has caused families to experience stress in trying to coordinate work and child care arrangements and has resulted in rising numbers of latchkey children. These children may be at risk for involvement in accidents and victimization, depending upon their age, characteristics, and environment.

C. How does television affect children?
(pp. 70–74; study goals 12–15)

Both correlational and experimental studies link heavy TV viewing with aggressive behavior in children and adults. However, Action for Children's Television and many parents are equally if not more concerned with *advertising* directed at children, which, they contend, exploits children's indiscriminate viewing habits and inability to judge the relative worth of products. These critics argue that such advertising encourages an attitude of continuous consumption. Although TV may increase the amount of time families spend together viewing programs, it may discourage conversation and is often used as a baby-sitter, intentionally employed to reduce family interaction. If used appropriately, on the other hand, TV can be a learning tool, capable of promoting prosocial behavior and exposing the average citizen to more information than ever before. However, unlike the print media, TV may present this information at a pace that does not permit much reflection. Some critics even argue that excessive amounts of passive viewing may decrease children's capacity for sustained attention and deliberate thought.

V. How can children's lives be improved?
   (pp. 74–81; study goals 16–18)

The family support program movement attempts to deal with the problems that demographic changes have caused for children by assisting the families that care for them. These programs, which include everything from information and referral services to day care and parent education, are often grass-roots self-help programs, initiated and run by those they serve.

Government's first major venture into family support was the Social Security Act of 1935, which offered financial assistance to the aged, the blind, and children in fatherless homes during the depression era. Today, Aid to Families with Dependent Children (AFDC), food stamps, and Medicaid are available to children in families with incomes below the poverty level. However, AFDC sustained sharp reductions in 1980, cuts which were accompanied by increased reports of requests for emergency food and shelter from private relief agencies. Though government assistance to families has traditionally concentrated on the poor, demographic changes may mean that assistance will need to be extended to other types of families.

How may we act to improve conditions for children and families? Social indicators and principles drawn from child development research (e.g., the *principle of integrity and continuity*) may be combined with the legal and fiscal expertise of lawmakers to design policies that facilitate family life. In addition, child development experts may help business executives to plan, implement, and evaluate changes in the workplace that facilitate family life (e.g., flexible work arrangements, job sharing, maternity leaves, child care facilities, and part-time opportunities). Experts and other child advocates may prevent or ameliorate conditions harmful to children and families by forming coalitions, encouraging awareness of children's and families' needs and problems, monitoring the conditions of children's lives, and disseminating research findings.

SIGNIFICANT CONCEPTS AND TOPICS

You should become familiar with and be able to explain the following concepts and topics. Most of the terms are highlighted in the margins of the text and some are also defined in the glossary at the end of the text.

childhood social indicators

demography

reconstituted families

latchkey children

Action for Children's Television (ACT)

Aid to Families with Dependent Children (AFDC)

advocacy

blended families

new extended families

continuous consumption

family support programs

facilitating family life

principle of integrity and continuity

SELF-CHECK

Choose the response that best answers the question or completes the statement.

_____ 1. In the early 1700s,
   a. children were considered in need of education and protection.
   b. childhood was considered a special period of the life cycle, qualitatively different from adulthood.
   c. there appears to have been no special emotional attachment to children.
   d. none of the above

_____ 2. Which of the following is *not* among recent demographic trends?
   a. smaller percentages of single parent families
   b. increasing percentages of young adults
   c. increasing percentages of older individuals
   d. decreasing percentages of children

_____ 3. Which of the following factors is *not* positively associated with the degree of children's ability to cope with divorce and post-divorce changes?
   a. the length of the parents' marriage
   b. the presence of siblings
   c. the psychological status of the custodial parent
   d. the child's age

_____ 4. Which of the following problems is most common among families in which both parents work outside the home?
   a. poverty
   b. depression
   c. stress in trying to coordinate work and child care arrangements
   d. problems with the management of child behavior

_____ 5. Complete the following sentence: Television may _____ the amount of time families spend together and _____ .
   a. decrease, encourage conversation
   b. increase, encourage conversation
   c. decrease, discourage conversation
   d. increase, discourage conversation

_____ 6. The principle of integrity and continuity
   a. is a description of the ideal characteristics of political succession.
   b. indicates that child advocates can be most effective by remaining separate and distinct from other interest groups and applying continuous pressure.
   c. states that children and families benefit if integrity and continuity of the family are maintained.
   d. none of the above

_____ 7. Family support programs
   a. are income subsidies.
   b. are virtually nonexistent in American society.
   c. assume that the family is the primary economic unit in modern society.
   d. emphasize that child development occurs in the context of the family.

13

_____ 8. The Social Security Act of 1935
   a. assisted the blind, the aged, and fatherless children.
   b. was an early family support program.
   c. both of the above
   d. none of the above
_____ 9. Action for Children's Television
   a. encourages TV producers to include more action in their child-directed programming.
   b. is a public relations unit supported by the television industry.
   c. is an example of a child advocacy group.
   d. none of the above
_____ 10. Which of the following statements is the most correct summary of research on maternal employment?
   a. There is a body of research that indicates that women's working outside the home results in their children having a higher incidence of behavioral problems.
   b. There is no body of research to indicate that women's working outside the home harms children.
   c. There is a body of research that indicates that the sons of mothers who stay at home are more obedient and perform slightly better in school than sons of working mothers.
   d. Research clearly indicates that maternal employment is associated with lower academic functioning among girls.

Answers to Self-Check Questions

1. c	**6.** c
2. a	**7.** d
3. a	**8.** c
4. c	**9.** c
5. d	**10.** b

OUR BIOLOGICAL HERITAGE

STUDY GOALS

After reading and studying Chapter 2, you should be able to:

1. Describe the relationship between genotype and phenotype, explaining such concepts as *range of reaction, critical periods,* and *canalization.*

2. Use Mendel's laws to explain the genetic transmission of recessive disorders and sex-linked recessive disorders, giving examples of each.

3. Describe the structural relationships among cells, nuclei, chromosomes, DNA, genes, bases, and RNA.

4. Name at least two sources of genetic variability and describe briefly how each works to enhance variation.

5. Compare and contrast genetic screening, diagnosis, and genetic counseling.

6. Explain the persistence of genes that cause life-threatening conditions, such as sickle cell anemia.

7. Contrast amniocentesis and chorion biopsy.

8. Discuss the medical, moral, legal, and ethical issues posed by the use of prenatal screening tests.

9. Describe the potential benefits and dangers of genetic engineering.

10. Summarize current attitudes toward the nature-nurture question.

11. Describe the advantages and disadvantages of using animal studies to investigate the relationship between behavior and genetic inheritance and explain how selective breeding is used.

12. List the assumptions on which twin studies of genetic influence are based and explain how to interpret differences in concordance rates between monozygotic and dizygotic twins.

13. Describe the assumptions that support studies of genetic influence using adoptees, and explain how to interpret differences in concordance rates between adoptees and their biological parents versus adoptees and their adoptive parents.

14. Discuss factors that may complicate the interpretation of adoptive and twin studies by violating their assumptions.

15. Summarize the research concerning the relationships between genetic inheritance, environmental factors, and intelligence.

16. Summarize the conclusions of research concerning the heritability of personality characteristics.

REVIEWING THE CHAPTER

I. How is genetic information stored and transmitted?
    (pp. 87–111; study goals 1–6)

We owe much of our understanding of genetics to the work of Gregor Mendel, who articulated principles of inheritance. Among these principles is that each gene has two alleles, one contributed by each parent, which behave in a pattern of dominance or recessiveness. In the heterozygous condition, it is the dominant allele that determines the phenotype—the observable characteristic associated with a particular genotype. The variety of different phenotypes that can arise from the same genotype depends on environmental factors and the range of reaction of the genotype in question. Sources which encourage variability among genotypes include genetic mutations and crossing over, in which some section of a chromosome breaks away and attaches to an adjacent chromosome during meiosis.

Since Mendel's time, molecular biologists have further clarified the nature of genes. Their work has shown that genes are sequences of bases in a DNA molecule located inside the cell's nucleus. DNA molecules compose the 46 chromosomes found in the normal human somatic cell, which may hold hundreds of thousands of genes. Unlike the somatic cells, which reproduce via mitosis, gametes, or reproductive cells, reproduce through a process called meiosis and contain only 23 chromosomes.

Better comprehension of the nature of genes and the processes through which they are reproduced have helped us understand how some diseases are inherited. Albinism and PKU, for example, are linked to the expression of a single, recessive gene. However, most characteristics and diseases are caused by polygenetic inheritance—several genes acting in concert and under certain environmental conditions. Karyotypes are used to identify chromosome abnormalities associated with several physical and behavioral defects. Through this process, Down's Syndrome has been traced to abnormalities in the 21st chromosome and Turner's and Klinefelter's Syndromes have been related to sex chromosome abnormalities.

The transmission or expression of many genetic defects can be prevented through genetic counseling and screening. Screening, accompanied by postscreening diagnostic evaluation is now used to detect such disorders as PKU, cystic fibrosis, sickle cell anemia, and Tay-Sachs disease. Though successful treatment is not available for all of these conditions, the phenotype normally associated with PKU can be avoided by employing dietary restrictions. By following such a regimen, an individual with the PKU genotype may become a phenocopy, whose observable characteristics mimic those of a person with another genotype.

II. What is the societal impact of our increasing knowledge of genetics? (pp. 111–114; study goals 7–9)

Our knowledge of genetics has enabled us to detect genetic abnormalities even before birth, through the use of amniocentesis and chorion biopsy. Table 2.1 summarizes the characteristics of these two prenatal screening tests.

Table 2.1   Characteristics of chorion biopsy and amniocentesis.

	Chorion Biopsy	Amniocentesis
Status	experimental	non-experimental; in wide use
Timing	given as early as the first month of pregnancy	given during the fourth month of pregnancy
Availability of results	ready in one day	ready in three weeks
Material sampled	chorion cells	amniotic fluid cells
Characteristics detected	genetic abnormalities and sex	genetic abnormalities and sex
Utility/Disadvantages	Chorion biopsy decreases stress and anxiety and minimizes the risks of abortion.	Should parents choose to abort, the procedure would be performed in the fifth month, when it is much riskier.

Medical, moral, legal, and ethical issues have been raised by the use of such tests. On the medical front, there is disagreement as to whether the risks the tests impose on mother and child are outweighed by their benefits. Moral and ethical questions are raised by the fact that most parents who learn that their child is genetically abnormal choose to abort even though the tests reveal nothing about the functional *severity* of such abnormalities. Some physicians refuse to perform amniocentesis because abortion may be called for. There is also some possibility of a live birth after a late abortion, which might leave a hospital open to legal claims of "wrongful life."

Sufficient progress in *genetic engineering* may one day permit us to synthesize or transplant genes to prevent many of the disorders identified by prenatal screening tests. For instance, *cloning,* the asexual reproduction of identical progeny, may lead to better understanding of chromosomes and their relationship to disease. It is argued that such genetic engineering should be regulated in order to minimize the likelihood of lab-created organisms being accidentally released in the environment and to reduce the possibility of unethical applications. However, much simpler techniques, such as the prenatal genetic screening tests, hold the potential for tampering with the genetic inheritance of the species by unbalancing the sex ratio or decreasing genetic variability.

III. What is the relationship between heredity and behavior?
(pp. 114–124; study goals 10–16)

The nature-nurture controversy was hotly debated for many years before researchers came to agree that, in its extreme form, the nature-nurture question is meaningless. The new consensus is that although there are no genes for behavior, genes act at a molecular level on the development and maintenance of structures that do have consequences for behavior. Recognizing that both heredity and environment are important, psychologists now ask, "In what way and to what extent do genetic and environmental factors interact to affect development and how does this interaction differ for specific behavioral traits?"

This question has been addressed by studies using animals, twins, and adopted children. Animal studies take advantage of the ease with which animals' environments can be manipulated and the relative simplicity of their behavior. In addition to varying environmental factors, animal studies employ selective breeding techniques to investigate the effects of heredity on behavioral traits. Although their results cannot be directly applied to humans, these studies demonstrate the potential effect of environmental factors on the expression of genetic inheritance and offer powerful demonstrations of the dictum that phenotype is determined by the interaction of the genotype and the environment.

Twin studies are based on two major assumptions. The first of these is that, if traits are highly genetically determined, then identical (monozygotic) twins should have identical traits. The second assumption made in twin studies is that environmental factors are equivalent for identical and fraternal twins reared together (i.e., environmental factors are no more encouraging of similarity between one type of twins than between the other type). This approach compares the concordance rates for a given trait between monozygotic and dizygotic twins. A higher concordance rate for monozygotic twins is taken to indicate genetic influence. High concordance rates between monozygotic twins reared apart provide especially impressive evidence of genetic influence. However, cases of separated identical twins are rare and it is even more unusual that their rearing environments are widely different.

Studies of adopted children investigate the role of genetics by comparing concordance rates between such children and their adoptive parents with concordance rates between adopted children and their biological parents. Higher concordance rates between adoptees and their biological parents are taken to indicate genetic influence. However, such comparisons are weakened by the tendency of adoption agencies to place children with couples similar to their biological parents.

The relationship between heredity and intelligence has proved difficult to study because of disagreements concerning the definition of intelligence and what intel-

18

ligence tests actually measure. Although the heritability ratio varies across traits and studies, it tends to be quite high for intelligence, indicating a substantial genetic contribution. Both twin and adoptive studies suggest that intelligence test performance is highly influenced by heredity and other work indicates that the correlation between individuals' IQs increases with the extent of their genetic similarity. Nonetheless, environmental factors have a substantial impact on intelligence; stimulating environments can increase the IQ of some infants and children and poor environments can lower the IQ.

Just as in the case of studies of intelligence and heredity, there are problems with studying the relationship between heredity and personality traits because of disagreements concerning how to define and measure such traits. However, there does appear to be a genetic influence on introversion and extroversion. In other respects, personality appears to be more heavily influenced by environmental factors than by genetic inheritance. Nonetheless, researchers studying identical twins reared apart have noticed similarities in gait, laughter and tone of voice, brain waves, abilities and interests, phobias, emotional styles, and vocational preferences. Some of these similarities have not been found in other studies and may be coincidental. However, twins reared apart have less need to affirm their individuality and it is plausible that this would permit their similarities to become more prominent than those between twins reared together.

SIGNIFICANT CONCEPTS, PEOPLE, AND TOPICS

You should become familiar with and be able to explain the following concepts, people, and topics. Most of the terms are highlighted in the margins of the text and some are also defined in the glossary at the end of the text.

gene-environment transactions	*genotype*
phenotype	*range of reaction*
transactional model of development	*critical period*
canalization	*preparedness*
Gregor Mendel	*gene*
alleles	*homozygous*
heterozygous	*dominance*
recessiveness	*Mendel's laws of inheritance*
albinism	*phenylketonuria (PKU)*
phenocopy	*carrier*
complex gene activity	*polygenetic inheritance*
pleitropy	*modifier genes*
cell	*cell wall*
cytoplasm	*nucleus*
structural genes	*operator genes*

regulator genes
chromosomes
deoxyribonucleic acid (DNA)
sugar phosphate molecules
adenine
cytosine
sperm cell
zygote
fetus
reproductive cells
mitosis
genetic variability
autosomes
hemophilia
Turner's syndrome
mutations
germinal mutations
Down's syndrome
nondisjunction
population gene pool
Tay-Sachs disease
genetic screening
chorion biopsy
genetic engineering
nature-nurture controversy
twin studies
monozygotic twins
dizygotic twins
adoption studies
heritability ratio

chromatin
gene locus
ribonucleic acid (RNA)
bases
thymine
guanine
ovum cell
embryo
gametes
somatic cells
meiosis
crossing over
sex-linked or X-linked recessive
  disorders
karyotype
Klinefelter's syndrome
somatic mutations
mutant genes
translocation
evolution
sickle cell anemia
genetic counseling
cystic fibrosis
amniocentesis
cloning
selective breeding
identical twins
fraternal twins
intrapair concordance

SELF-CHECK

Choose the response that best answers the question or completes the statement.

_____ 1. Canalized behaviors
  a. are innate.
  b. are easily modified after they've been acquired.
  c. are easily learned.
  d. are highly vulnerable to environmental influence.

_____ 2. Translocation and nondisjunction of chromosomes have been implicated in
  a. Down's syndrome.
  b. sickle cell anemia.
  c. PKU.
  d. hemophilia.

_____ 3. A researcher finds that the concordance rate for trait *A* is twice as high between monozygotic twins as it is between dizygotic twins. She would probably conclude that
  a. there is little genetic influence on the exhibition of trait *A*.
  b. there may be a substantial genetic influence on the exhibition of trait *A*.
  c. the study is inconclusive.
  d. the results rule out the possibility of a substantial environmental contribution to trait *A*.

_____ 4. Gregor Mendel
  a. was an early biologist who argued that hereditary transmission was accomplished through a mixing of blood.
  b. articulated laws of genetic inheritance derived from the study of the pea plant.
  c. was the originator of evolutionary theory.
  d. expounded the principle of survival of the fittest.

_____ 5. *Unlike* amniocentesis, chorion biopsy
  a. can only be performed during the fourth month of pregnancy.
  b. can provide results within one day of testing.
  c. is capable of detecting a baby's sex.
  d. is a non-experimental procedure in fairly widespread use.

_____ 6. If both alleles give the same hereditary direction for a certain trait, an individual is said to be _____ for that trait.
  a. monozygotic
  b. dizygotic
  c. heterozygous
  d. homozygous

_____ 7. PKU and albinism are both examples of
  a. phenocopies.
  b. canalization.
  c. conditions transmitted by a recessive gene.
  d. genetic translocation.

_____ 8. Assume that eye color is transmitted by a single gene and that the brown allele is dominant. If two brown-eyed individuals that are heterozygous for this trait (both BROWN-blue) should conceive children, which of the following would be true of their offspring according to Mendel's Laws?
   a. They would be brown-eyed.
   b. They would be blue-eyed.
   c. They would have a 25% chance of being blue-eyed.
   d. They would have a 50% chance of being brown-eyed.

_____ 9. A trait with a wide range of reaction
   a. is largely genetically determined.
   b. is transmitted by a dominant gene.
   c. is highly responsive to environmental variation.
   d. is said to be canalized.

_____ 10. A *phenocopy* is
   a. an individual whose observable characteristic has been environmentally altered to mimic those usually associated with another specific genotype.
   b. a clone.
   c. the product of pleitropy.
   d. a product of genetic engineering.

Answers to Self-Check Questions

1. c		**6.** d	
2. a		**7.** c	
3. b		**8.** c	
4. b		**9.** c	
5. b		**10.** a	

PRENATAL DEVELOPMENT AND BIRTH

STUDY GOALS

After reading and studying Chapter 3, you should be able to:

1. Explain what happens to the egg immediately upon fertilization and know some of the barriers to fertilization.

2. Know the three stages of prenatal development and the developmental processes that occur during each of these stages.

3. Understand the functions of auxiliary structures—the placenta, the umbilical cord, and the amniotic sac.

4. Understand the notion of the age of viability and explain why the age of viability may be periodically revised.

5. Define the term *critical period* and explain why the prenatal period is considered a critical developmental period.

6. Define the term *teratogen* and explain why the study of the effects of teratogens and other factors that influence prenatal development is important.

7. Understand why there are variations in the degree to which the influences of teratogens or other environmental factors will culminate in developmental abnormalities and define the two notions used to explain these variations.

8. Know the difference between teratogens and other factors that influence prenatal development and explain the specific damage that each teratogen or other influencing factor may cause to the developing fetus.

9. Understand the importance of maternal nutrition during pregnancy and the effects of malnutrition on brain growth.

10. Discuss the relationship between poverty and reproductive outcome.

11. Describe the Supplemental Food Program for Women, Infants, and Children and discuss its importance.

12. Understand the birth process and discuss the risk factors involved.

13. Understand the difference between premature and low-birth-weight babies and explain the difficulties experienced by these babies and their parents.

14. Discuss current developments in birthing that have arisen out of concern for the psychological needs of the mother.

15. Understand the social factors related to pregnancy and birth and explain how they can influence the life of the child.

16. Understand the known causes of infertility as these relate to men and women and explain the solutions and treatments for infertility and the legal, moral, and ethical implications of these.

REVIEWING THE CHAPTER

I. What are the stages of prenatal development?
    (pp. 127–132; study goals 1–4)

Immediately upon fertilization the ovum (now known as the zygote) establishes itself in the thickened lining of the uterus and prenatal development proceeds. There are three stages to prenatal development: the period of the ovum, the period of the embryo, and the period of the fetus. During each of these periods the organism undergoes a number of changes, including the formation of solid bone (ossification), differentiation of important organs, and the development of auxiliary structures which serve to support the organism. These auxiliary structures are the placenta, which allows for the passage of substances from the maternal bloodstream to that of the fetus; the amniotic sac, which contains a fluid that protects the fetus; and the umbilical cord, which gives the growing fetus flexibility of movement and facilitates the pumping of blood to and from the fetal heart.

During the prenatal period, the fetus maintains a physiologically dependent relationship with the mother. By the end of 26 to 28 weeks after conception, a time referred to as the age of viability, fetal development is sufficiently advanced so that if birth occurs, the organism will survive. If birth occurs before this time, the nervous and respiratory system of the fetus are not mature enough to allow for survival outside the uterine environment. Although the age of viability is currently set at 26 to 28 weeks, this may be revised as medical advances allow for the survival of infants born before that time.

II. What are the environmental influences on prenatal development?
    (pp. 132–147; study goals 5–11)

The prenatal period is known as a critical developmental period because during this time the fetus is vulnerable to a variety of environmental influences which could result in physical and/or mental abnormalities. However, not all fetuses are equally vulnerable. The effects of such environmental influences may vary depending on the time during the prenatal period that they occur and the genetic predisposition of the mother and the fetus. Conditions after birth are also important. The human infant has a strong, innate self-righting mechanism so that although 10% of all children are born with some kind of a handicap, many of these handicaps decrease with age or entirely disappear. However, if a child is influenced by adverse factors before birth as well as after birth, the likelihood that the handicap will disappear is reduced significantly. For this reason psychologists are particularly concerned with children who are poor because they may not only suffer from adverse influences during the prenatal period, they are also likely to suffer after they are born from conditions associated with poverty such as inferior sanitation and shelter, lack of adequate health care, and malnutrition.

Several adverse environmental influences to prenatal development have been identified. Some of these are known as teratogens, which cause damage to developing but not yet fully formed organs. The word *teratogen* is derived from the Greek work *teras,* which means monster. Examples of teratogens are radiation and chemicals, drugs taken by the mother (including medication, caffeine, nicotine, alcohol, and illegal drugs). Besides the adverse influence of teratogens, the fetus is also subject to other environmental factors. These include diseases contracted by the mother, the mother's age, the mother's emotions (for example, if the mother is under a great deal of stress or suffers from depression or anxiety), and the mother's diet.

The mother's diet is especially important during the prenatal period because it has a direct influence on the growth of the brain. Studies which involved autopsies of malnourished animals and children suggest that malnutrition during the prenatal period leads to deficits in brain weight at birth and to a decrease in the number of brain cells. Given the importance of nutrition during pregnancy, a government-sponsored program known as the Supplemental Food Program for Women, Infants, and Children (popularly known as the WIC Program) has been developed. The program ensures that low-income pregnant women, infants, and young children receive the nutrients they need to grow up physically and mentally healthy. Evaluations of the WIC Program have demonstrated its effectiveness. They have shown that children from low-income families whose mothers participated in the program during pregnancy have higher cognitive functioning and behavioral adaptation during their preschool years than those children from low-income families whose mothers did not participate in WIC.

III. Are there risks to childbirth?
(pp. 148–163; study goals 12–16)

Although a number of environmental factors have been identified as being potentially dangerous during the prenatal period, most of the time pregnancy is a normal event that proceeds without complications as long as the pregnant woman receives adequate and regular prenatal care. The birth process is also a normal uncomplicated event for most women. However, childbirth still carries some risks.

Some women suffer extreme anxiety during the last stages of pregnancy and through labor and delivery. Such anxiety complicates the birth process and may result in abnormalities in the child. Because the psychological status of the mother is an important factor that is likely to influence the newborn baby, several practices have been instituted to help mothers overcome their anxiety and make the birth a happier and healthier event for the parents and the baby. One such practice is natural childbirth. Another is the Lamaze method. Both these practices prepare the mother for labor and delivery and teach her techniques that will facilitate the birth. Another practice that is enjoying increasing popularity is gentle birthing. In gentle birthing the baby is delivered in a dimly lit and relatively quiet room and is gently placed on the mother's abdomen while the umbilical cord is cut. Many hospitals also make provisions for rooming in, a practice wherein the baby and the mother stay in the same room after delivery. This enables the mother and baby to become better acquainted with one another. Although many mothers opt for rooming in, others prefer their entry to parenthood to be a little more gradual so they request that the hospital assume primary care of the baby during the first day or two after birth.

During the birth process, the two major dangers to the infant are (1) pressures on the head, which may cause brain hemorrhaging, and (2) insufficient oxygen, which, if severe, can result in cerebral palsy.

Some babies may also be born prematurely or they may be born on time, but they may be of low birth weight. Full-term low-birth-weight babies are physically mature enough to breathe and suck normally after birth whereas premature babies are not. However, low birth weight is considered to be a more serious condition because it suggests that fetal development has been impaired and there may be a permanently slow rate of development. Preterm babies, on the other hand, continue to develop after birth although they need intensive care until they gain sufficient weight.

Both preterm and low-birth-weight babies are vulnerable and may be lethargic and slow to respond and develop. Although in many cases these babies will eventually attain normal development they may have difficulty establishing an affectionate relationship with their parents and their parents may suffer extreme frustration and anxiety having to take care of an unresponsive and developmentally delayed and vulnerable infant. For this reason, psychologists suggest that the parents receive help and support as they cope with the care of their baby.

Not only parents of premature and low-birth-weight infants, but all parents need support in the first few weeks of the infant's life. Many also need to be taught what to expect of infants at different ages as many of them have unrealistic expectations of what infants are capable of. For this reason, many secondary schools and hospitals have instituted parenting education programs for would-be and new parents.

Such programs are considered to be important because today, young couples are separated from their extended families, and they have no means by which to learn from others about the care of a newborn baby. Some parents today are single parents who have chosen to be clinically inseminated with sperm from a donor in order to conceive. This brings us to the question of why people have children. Psychologists who have investigated this question note that the reasons for having children differ according to culture and the social climate and economy of a particular society. Whereas in developing countries people have children because they value the support of children, in our society many parents have children because they feel children bring happiness and joy and that they are fun to play with.

Approximately 20% of couples wishing to have children cannot conceive. Infertility can stem from problems related to the man or woman. In 10 to 20% of the cases, no cause for infertility can be found. Infertility can be an emotionally traumatic experience for the couple especially now that there are few babies being given up for adoption. However, there are some medical procedures that can help infertile couples. These include artificial insemination, test-tube babies, egg transplant, and surrogate womb. These procedures have helped many couples, but they are associated with legal, moral, and ethical considerations which are difficult to resolve.

SIGNIFICANT CONCEPTS, PEOPLE, AND TOPICS

You should become familiar with and be able to explain the following concepts, people, and topics. Most of the terms are highlighted in the margins of the text and some are also defined in the glossary at the end of the text.

ovum	*zygote*
capacitation	*decidua*
amniotic sac	*amniotic fluid*
chorion	*period of the ovum*
period of the embryo	*period of the fetus*
ossification	*ectoderm*
mesoderm	*endoderm*
placenta	*villi*
intervillus space	*umbilical cord*
age of viability	*critical period*
teratogens	*continuum of reproductive casualty*
continuum of caretaking casualty	*thalidomide*
phocomelia	*DES*
fetal alcohol syndrome	*rubella*
toxemia	*RH factor*
brain growth spurts	*myelination*
infant mortality	*the WIC program*
Apgar scoring system	*natural childbirth*
Lamaze method	*gentle birthing*
rooming in	*birthing rooms*
anoxia	*cerebral palsy*

preterm or *premature baby*
minimal brain dysfunction
infertility
test tube babies
surrogate womb
Frederick LeBoyer

full-term, low-birth-weight baby
apnea
donor sperm
egg transplant
Virginia Apgar

SELF-CHECK

Choose the response that best answers the question or completes the statement.

_____ 1. In order for conception to occur between the ovum and sperm, intercourse must take place within _____ days of ovulation.
    a. three
    b. five
    c. two
    d. none of the above

_____ 2. In the first moments of the union between ovum and sperm the _____ is formed and the process of cell division begins.
    a. gamete
    b. fetus
    c. amnion
    d. zygote

_____ 3. Most spontaneous abortions occur
    a. during the period of the ovum.
    b. at about three months gestation.
    c. at about four months gestation.
    d. during the period of the embryo.

_____ 4. During the _____ , organ systems begin to form.
    a. embryo period
    b. fetal period
    c. ovum period
    d. conception period

_____ 5. The zygote differentiates into three layers. Identify which layer the zygote does not differentiate into.
    a. endoderm
    b. mesoderm
    c. ectoderm
    d. metaderm

_____ 6. The _____ is the organ through which substances pass from the mother to the developing organism.
    a. chorion
    b. amniotic sac
    c. placenta
    d. villi

_____ 7. The age of viability occurs _____ weeks after conception.
    a. 36–37
    b. 32–34
    c. 26–28
    d. 14–16

_____ 8. A critical period in prenatal development is
   a. the time when the developing organism is most likely to abort.
   b. the number of weeks the developing fetus needs to stay within the womb.
   c. the time at which intercourse needs to take place for successful conception.
   d. the time in which the organism is especially sensitive to a particular substance.

_____ 9. Identify which substance *cannot* cross the placental barrier.
   a. caffeine
   b. nicotine
   c. drugs
   d. None, all can cross the placental barrier.

_____ 10. Fertilization usually takes place in the _____ .
   a. cervix
   b. fallopian tubes
   c. uterus
   d. ovary

Answers to Self-Check Questions

1. c	**6.** c
2. d	**7.** c
3. d	**8.** d
4. a	**9.** d
5. d	**10.** b

CHAPTER 4

PHYSICAL DEVELOPMENT DURING INFANCY

STUDY GOALS

After reading and studying Chapter 4, you should be able to:

1. Appreciate the interaction of genetic and environmental influences (nature–nurture) in the course of physical and psychological development of the infant.

2. Understand how the human baby is at the same time both dependent and competent.

3. Understand the evolutionary and adaptive significance of infant reflexes and later voluntary actions that the infant develops.

4. Know the difference between infant sensory and perceptual abilities and have a working knowledge of the specific capacities the infant possesses.

5. Describe the role of infant state on infant behavior and learning.

6. Discuss the role of habituation and dishabituation as the silent language of infants in understanding how and what infants respond to in the environment.

7. Describe the various visual capacities the infant possesses: visual scanning, perceiving different patterns and shapes, preferences for the human face, and depth perception.

8. Discuss the individual, gender, and cross-cultural differences that infants possess in regard to infant crying, ability to be calmed, and activity level and temperament. Understand how each influences the infant-caregiver relationship.

9. Describe the three parts of the brain, when they mature, and the functions they control.

10. Understand the developmental functions and changes in REM sleep for the infant.

11. Describe the numerous changes in the infant's physical growth, motor development and maturation, and two principles that govern this process.

31

12. Understand the changes in the infant's brain development and the implications for psychological development.

13. Appreciate that as knowledge about infant capacities has grown, one indirect result has been a growing emphasis on the part of parents and our culture to overemphasize learning and cognitive stimulation programs for the infant.

14. Discuss the interactive roles of maturation and environmental stimulation or deprivation in the infant's motor development.

REVIEWING THE CHAPTER

I. What is the newborn baby all about?
(pp. 169–188; study goals 1, 2, 3, 5, 8, 10)

Since the 1960s, we have learned a great deal from psychologists' research about what newborns know when they emerge into this world and what they are capable of. The implications of this research challenge our perceptions about the newborn, how they should be raised, and what we might expect of them. Yet, in spite of this competence we are aware that at the same time newborns are dependent on adults for physical care and nurture. The newborn's appearance is often termed "quite odd" because of the strong contrast to the appearance of older babies and the disproportion among various parts of his body. The newborn is also born with a repertoire of involuntary reflexes (e.g.: rooting, sucking) which ensure survival and adaptive functioning in his environment. Many of the reflexes such as the Moro reflex disappear within two to three months, and others such as the stepping and grasping reflexes reveal neurological apparatus that is later used for voluntary actions such as walking and grasping.

Investigators have also found that along with the predictable and orderly sequences of infant growth and development, there are individual differences among babies. Evidence indicates there are cross-cultural and gender differences in the amount infants cry, their ability to be calmed, and in their activity levels. The seminal work of Thomas et al. on temperamental traits has allowed us to identify differences in behavioral styles in infants (easy, slow-to-warm-up, and difficult) and to understand how these styles interact with environmental variables and caregiving styles. Work on infant states (degrees of wakefulness and sleep) by Brazelton and his colleagues has been instrumental in understanding the internal mechanisms which influence individual and developmental differences in the newborn's physiological competence. We now know that in order to benefit from the environment, the infant needs to be in a quiet, alert state, for in this state his sensory and perceptual pathways are open. Understanding individual differences in their infant is important information for the parents to know because it affects their interaction and relationship with the infant and the type of environment the infant is exposed to.

II. What are the sensory and perceptual capabilities of the infant?
(pp. 188–202; study goals 4, 6, 7, 13)

As a result of the vast interest by psychologists in the abilities of the newborn and developing infant, we now know that this very youngest of human beings actively interacts with her environment from the first days of life and knows more than we used to think. The newborn arrives in this world with the ability to see, hear, taste, smell, and respond to touch. The infant has the ability to detect a certain stimulus in the environment (sensation) and also the ability to process or interpret the sensations (perception). Although these sensory and perceptual abilities are immature at birth, they very quickly become more refined and differentiated as the infant grows and develops. Because the infant cannot use verbal or motor responses as older children and adults can to respond to various stimuli, researchers have had to use the responses the infant can make, such as change in heart rate, sucking, and looking time as measures of infant responsiveness. Researchers rely on two techniques, habituation and dishabituation to interpret their results. Habituation is a type of learning which indicates that a particular stimulus has become familiar, or learned, and thus no longer elicits interest. Dishabituation reveals that the infant can discriminate among objects and remembers what she has seen in the past.

Numerous studies indicate the human infant is very responsive to human vocalization. Very quickly the infant prefers a female voice to the sound of a bell and can come to recognize and prefer her own mother's voice to a stranger's voice. A baby as young as one to two months old is able to hear the difference between similar sounds such as "pa" and "ba." The infant's responsivity to touch is evidenced by her reflex responses and the fact that a crying baby usually can be soothed by being held or picked up.

The infant's visual capabilities are the most developed of the five senses and have been the most widely investigated. We now know that newborns are sensitive to bright lights and can focus on objects or people within a close range. The ability to focus at a distance becomes refined with age. Psychologists have also discovered that infants prefer to look at normal human faces and colored patterns rather than plain colors or objects with no patterns. Infants also develop strategies for looking and these strategies change with development. In numerous studies employing the visual cliff, psychologists have found that infants as young as three months have some idea of depth. It is believed that this innate mechanism serves an evolutionary purpose in protecting the young from falling.

With all that has been discovered about infant capabilities, one of the unfortunate consequences has been the quest for developing the superbaby. The result has been an emphasis on early stimulation and reading programs for infants. Parents are told to give their infant as many stimulating experiences as possible and to do it as early in life as possible. The question is not whether stimulation is or is not important. We know stimulation is important, but rather in what amounts, in what ways, and at what point in the infant's development should it be provided?

III. How does the infant grow and develop?
(pp. 202–215; study goals 9, 11, 12, 14)

Along with all the other aspects of the infant's development, physical and motor growth also occurs very rapidly. Although there are individual differences in rate of growth, this process follows a predictable and orderly sequence which is governed by innate or genetic influences and the infant's interaction with the environment. The course of physical development has both direct and indirect influences on psychological development. Two principles govern physical growth: (1) growth occurs from head to toe (cephalocaudal), and (2) growth also occurs from near to far (proximodistal).

The physical growth of the brain within the first two years of life has vast implications for psychological and intellectual functioning. The three parts of the brain, the forebrain, the midbrain, and the hindbrain, mature at different times and have separate functions, which range, respectively, from breathing to emotions to intellectual behavior.

During the period of infancy, the baby changes from the newborn who is born with only reflex actions to the older infant who is able to accomplish a sequence of motor tasks which culminate in the integration of complex motor patterns and skills such as walking and grasping. These changes are dependent on brain maturation and increases in motor strength, which occur during infancy. This process is called *hierarchic integration*. Although the sequence of motor development is constant, the rate at which a particular skill develops varies from child to child.

An important component of the physical and motor development in infancy is the process of maturation. *Maturation* refers to the orderly physiological changes that occur independent of learning. The question of nature and nurture arises: How much of what infants can do is the result of innate, biological or maturational factors or the result of environmental input such as stimulation or training? The answer is not an either or situation, but rather reflects the belief that an interaction between biological and environmental characteristics needs to occur for optimal development of the infant.

SIGNIFICANT CONCEPTS, PEOPLE, AND TOPICS

You should become familiar with and be able to explain the following concepts, people, and topics. Most of the terms are highlighted in the margins of the text and some are also defined in the glossary at the end of the text.

newborn	*lanugo*
temperament	*reflexes*
Moro	*rooting*
grasping	*stepping*
Babinski	*infant state*

34

REM sleep
sensation
habituation
visual acuity
cross-modal transfer of information
retractive-inhibitive
proximodistal
neuralgia
axons
forebrain
hindbrain
hierarchic integration
sudden infant death syndrome (SIDS)
T. B. Brazelton

autostimulation
perception
dishabituation
visual cliff
reactive-expressive
cephalocaudal
neurons
glial cells
dendrites
midbrain
central nervous system
maturation
Chess and Thomas
Robert Fantz

SELF-CHECK

Choose the response that best answers the question or completes the statement.

_____ 1. Mothers report that there usually is a period of adjustment for both themselves and their babies and that they begin to feel comfortable in caring for the baby _____ after the baby is born.
   a. 2 to 4 weeks
   b. 2 to 6 weeks
   c. 6 to 8 weeks
   d. 7 to 12 weeks

_____ 2. Unlike the older infant, the newborn has the following physical characteristics.
   a. broad, flat face
   b. lanugo
   c. disproportionately large head, often misshapen
   d. a & b
   e. a, b, & c

_____ 3. Although the infant is dependent, it has also been said that he is not a competent human being who has innate capabilities for survival.
   a. true
   b. false

_____ 4. Temperament research has shown that temperament can be described as
   a. the foundation for later personality development.
   b. how the infant responds to the environment.
   c. a way of describing an infant's anger.
   d. a & b
   e. a, b, & c

_____ 5. Researchers have found that female babies cry less and are more easily pacified than male babies, but are also less active and awake for shorter periods of time.
   a. true
   b. false

_____ 6. The Thomas et al. longitudinal study of infant temperament resulted in the following categories for infants.
   a. quiet, average, active
   b. easy, slow-to-warm-up, difficult
   c. quiet, average, difficult
   d. easy, slow-to-warm-up, active

_____ 7. The rooting reflex is important for the infant
   a. for grasping.
   b. during feeding.
   c. for walking.
   d. none of the above

36

_____ 8. In order for the infant to learn, he needs to be in a(n) _____ state.
    a. quiet, alert
    b. stimulated
    c. quiet, calm
    d. calm

_____ 9. Robert is a 2-month-old infant who is being taken along to a large family gathering. With all the people, noise, and activity Robert may respond by
    a. looking away.
    b. crying.
    c. falling asleep.
    d. a and b
    e. a, b, or c

_____ 10. An infant spends _____ time in dreaming sleep than an adult.
    a. more
    b. the same amount of
    c. less

Answers to Self-Check Questions

1. b	**6.** b
2. e	**7.** b
3. b	**8.** a
4. d	**9.** e
5. a	**10.** a

CHAPTER 5

COGNITIVE AND LANGUAGE DEVELOPMENT DURING INFANCY

STUDY GOALS

After reading and studying Chapter 5, you should be able to:

1. Understand that both genetic and environmental factors influence the course of cognitive and language development.

2. Discuss the current research on infant perceptual development and explain how new research methods have contributed to our understanding of infants' capabilities.

3. Know the two major movements in perceptual development research and the seminal work of Robert Fantz and Eleanor and James Gibson.

4. Discuss what researchers know about infants' ability to remember and some of the ways researchers study memory in infancy.

5. Know the types of learning that have been investigated with infants and the conclusions derived from the research on infant learning.

6. Discuss the controversy that surrounds the study of imitation in infants and the theoretical explanations offered by researchers on either side of the controversy.

7. Define *cognition* and understand the significance of Jean Piaget's theory of cognitive development, as well as some of the limitations of his work.

8. Be familiar with the definitions of terms Piaget used to explain his theory—*cognitive structures, schemes, adaptation, assimilation, accommodation,* and *equilibrium.*

9. Understand the major tenet of Piaget's theory which is that the individual is an active organism who acquires cognitive skills as she interacts with the environment. Be able to explain the two inherent tendencies—organization and adaptation—that govern the individual's interaction with the environment.

10. Know the ages and basic characteristics associated with the four periods of cognitive development outlined in Piaget's theory—the sensorimotor, preoperational, concrete operations, and formal operations periods.

38

11. Know the six substages of the sensorimotor period of cognitive development and explain how thinking in infants differs from thinking as it is generally known.

12. Understand the different explanations offered as to how children acquire the ability to understand and speak language, and describe the views of B. F. Skinner, Noam Chomsky, and Eric Lenneberg.

13. Understand the difference between receptive and expressive (or productive) language skills.

14. Describe the milestones of language development during infancy and understand that these occur in an invariant order even though the age at which each milestone is acquired may differ from child to child.

15. Define the two characteristics of early speech—holophrasic speech and telegraphic speech.

16. Discuss the facts and myths associated with the current trend among parents to teach infants to read and the negative impact this can have on the baby.

17. Discuss the research on environmental deprivation and its effects on infant growth and development, and explain the role parents play in facilitating cognitive growth.

18. Discuss what is known from the research about the effects of day care on cognitive development, the limitations inherent in the research, and the factors associated with quality care for infants and the need to regulate day care facilities.

REVIEWING THE CHAPTER

I. Do infant's have the ability to perceive and learn?
(pp. 219–226; study goals 1–6)

The study of infancy in general, and of the infant's cognitive skills in particular, is enjoying a great deal of popularity among developmental psychologists. As new techniques are being devised by which to study very young infants, researchers are becoming increasingly impressed with the infant's ability to learn and with her delight in learning.

One of the most significant areas of the research is the work on perceptual development in infancy. There are two aspects to this work, the research on infants' sensory capabilities (discussed in the previous chapter), pioneered by Robert Fantz, and the work by Eleanor and James Gibson and others on the infant's ability to perceive objects, people, places, and events. These researchers are interested not only in whether or what infants can see or hear, but also, in how infants perceive what they see and hear. (For example, Do they know that the voice they hear is part of a configuration of mouth, eyes, and nose that make up the human face?) The research in this regard is important for it takes researchers one step closer toward eventually understanding whether the ways the human infant structures her world are innate or learned. So far, the research is inconclusive, but some researchers suggest that the infant may be born with organizing principles which enable her to perceive the environment and acquire more and more information.

Researchers have also studied the infant's ability to remember, and they note that babies as young as 2 to 4 weeks can remember a word they have heard repeatedly. However, infants can remember only those words which they repeatedly hear, but they cannot at this age remember other words, even their own nam ;, that are not subject to intensive repetition.

The fact that infants remember implies that they are learning. Two types of learning have been experimentally investigated with infants—classical conditioning and operant conditioning. Researchers have demonstrated that both classical and operant conditioning are means by which children learn. Studies on classical conditioning in infancy are difficult to conduct so the findings are as yet inconclusive. However, studies on operant conditioning in early infancy reveal not only that infants can be conditioned, but also, that the younger they are, the more time it takes them to become conditioned—a concept researchers refer to as *learning readiness*.

Learning can also occur through observation and imitation. Infants as young as 2 weeks of age have been found to imitate certain facial expressions. However, the research on imitation in infancy is controversial. At issue is not whether the infants had been observed to imitate or not. Rather, the issue is whether what is observed can be called true imitation. In true imitation, a child can imitate a behavior and in this way learn a new behavior. Young infants have been observed to imitate only those behaviors which are within their behavioral repertoire, so they are not actually learning a new behavior. Despite this fact, some researchers contend that the ability to imitate is innate, hence the finding that very young infants can imitate. Other researchers contend that what has been found is not true imitation because this skill is not innate but is acquired over time.

II. What are the contributions of Jean Piaget's theory of cognitive development? (pp. 226–237; study goals 7–11)

Although the research on perceptual development in infancy is currently enjoying great popularity, researchers owe a great deal of their understanding about infants' cognition to the work of Jean Piaget.

Jean Piaget has dominated the field of developmental psychology until recently. Currently researchers are finding that Piaget may have underestimated the abilities of infants and young children for two major reasons. One, he did not have available to him the innovative research tools researchers currently use, and two, he may have underestimated the importance of perceptual learning on cognitive growth. Despite these limitations in his work, Piaget is noted for his contributions to the field.

One of the major contributions Piaget has made is his revelation that the individual, from infancy through adulthood, is an active organism who constantly explores the environment, in the process acquiring knowledge. According to Piaget it is through the interaction between the individual and the environment that cognitive development occurs.

Another significant contribution Piaget has made is related to his assertion that cognitive development is a continuous process that occurs over four periods—the sensorimotor, preoperational, concrete operations, and formal operations periods. These periods occur in an invariant order and each lays the groundwork for the next. Each of these periods is also associated with a different way of understanding the environment. Thus, Piaget noted that children not only know more as they grow older, their way of thinking and understanding the environment actually changes with age.

During the first two years of life, the sensorimotor period of cognitive development, the infant learns by acting on the environment, using her sensory and motor capabilities such as seeing, touching, grasping, reaching, and sucking. The infant understands objects only through the actions she performs on them as it is not until the end of the period that she attains the ability to retain a mental picture "in her head," so to speak. It is also during this period that the infant gradually acquires *object permanence*—the ability to understand that objects continue to exist even though one cannot see, touch, or smell them directly.

Piaget maintained that although much of cognitive growth occurs according to an innate maturational timetable, experience with objects and people in the environment is vital to cognitive progress.

III. How do infants learn to speak?
(pp. 247–248; study goals 12–15)

Just as cognitive development is dependent both on maturation and experience, so language development is influenced by both biological and environmental factors. Although most researchers now know this, two opposing views on language development were proposed. One is the learning theory view espoused by B. F. Skinner. This view underscores the fact that infants learn language through reinforcement; when the baby babbles or utters a word, her parents are so delighted that their delight motivates the child to continue to utter the same sound or word. As she grows older, the child learns to speak because her parents and other people continually correct her and reinforce the appropriate speech.

Research studies have substantiated the fact that reinforcement is indeed an important aspect in learning to speak. But, as Noam Chomsky and Eric Lenneberg maintain, biological factors are also important and it appears that human beings possess an innate ability to produce speech sounds. In support of the biological explanation of language development, researchers further note that all normal infants go through several milestones as they acquire language. These milestones occur in an invariant order during the first two years of life and include the ability to produce early sounds, including crying, cooing, and babbling; the use of one word at a time; and finally, combining two or more words.

Researchers note, however, that although infants understand words that are spoken to them (receptive language ability) and they are able to produce words (expressive language ability), there is no indication that a word spoken by the infant has the same meaning to the infant as it does to an adult. For example, a baby may point to a horse and say "doggie." It is suggested that the infant is not

41

simply making a mistake when she refers to a horse as the doggie. Rather, she is generalizing on the basis of previous experience and reasons: I know this isn't a dog, but I don't know what it is, and it looks like a dog."

Infants also use single words to express ideas that adults would use a sentence to express (e.g., they say "me" to mean "I want to do it myself"), a phenomenon known as *holophrasic speech,* and they use words sparingly, in much the same way that adults use words sparingly when they send a telegram, a characteristic that is referred to as *telegraphic speech.*

IV. What has been learned from research on cognitive development?
(pp. 248–259; study goals 16–18)

The research on child development has practical applications and it is naturally of interest to parents, teachers, child caregivers, nurses, physicians, and others who interact with or who work with children. For this reason, findings from the research are invariably distributed to the general public.

Although there is value in explaining to parents and others some of the findings from the research, there is the danger that parents will be misled. For example, the research on the cognitive capabilities of infants has filtered to the popular media, exciting parents and other adults and alerting them to the amazing skills of newborn infants and their ability to perceive, remember, and even imitate at such a young age. At the same time, new "how-to" and "step-by-step" books and programs are being advertised telling parents to capitalize on the skills of infants and teach them to read or do math at the age of two. Parents are so bombarded by the advertising on ways that they can increase their infants' brain power that even well-meaning parents who shy away from such products are wondering if they may be depriving their children in some way.

The emphasis on teaching babies to read and acquire other academic skills is a contemporary example of previous efforts which saw the mind as a *tabula rasa* ready to be shaped by the environment. However, we know from the research that this is not the case. In quest of an answer to the nature-nurture question, researchers have found that a certain amount of environmental stimulation is necessary if development is to proceed normally, but that no amount of stimulation can change the genetic potential of the child. Rather than spend time "teaching" their baby, parents are advised to simply enjoy their child and spend time talking to and playing with her. It is on the basis of naturally occurring stimulating experiences that children thrive.

The fact that children need to have adults play with and talk to them is evident from the research that has been done with infants in institutions. When such infants are given only physical care but are deprived of interactions with a nurturant adult, they grow up retarded in their cognitive and language skills.

Since many infants today are in out-of-home care, there is concern that they may suffer developmental deficits as well. From the studies that have been done, we can conclude that infants who are in a high quality day care center do not suffer any negative effects and some infants, notably those from economically disadvantaged families, may even benefit from the day care experience.

However, most infants are not in day care centers but rather, in family day care homes. It is not known whether these settings are good or bad because there are currently no federal quality standards for the regulation of day care centers and day care homes.

SIGNIFICANT CONCEPTS, PEOPLE, AND TOPICS

You should become familiar with and be able to explain the following concepts, people, and topics. Most of the terms are highlighted in the margins of the text and some are also defined in the glossary at the end of the text.

productive memory
operant conditioning
interstimulus interval
cognition
preoperational period
formal operations period
active organism
organization
assimilation
equilibrium
representational thought
language acquisition device
deep structure
receptive language
telegraphic speech
family day care home
Eleanor and James Gibson
B. F. Skinner
Eric Lenneberg

classical conditioning
learning readiness
pseudo-imitation
sensorimotor period
concrete operations period
cognitive structures
schemes
adaptation
accommodation
object permanence
deferred imitation
surface structure
expressive language
holophrasic speech
day care center
Robert Fantz
Jean Piaget
Noam Chomsky

SELF-CHECK

Choose the response that best answers the question or completes the statement.

___ 1. Infants as young as _____ have knowledge that an object exists distinct and separate from other objects.
   a. 6 weeks
   b. 5 months
   c. 3 months
   d. 6 months

___ 2. Spelke's research on object perception suggests that infants _____ organizing principles that allow them to perceive objects.
   a. learn
   b. are born with

___ 3. Your older brother and his wife have just had a baby. They talk to her all the time, saying her name repeatedly to her. However, they are not sure this makes any difference to their daughter. As a psychologist you tell them that saying her name does have an impact on her learning for infants as young as _____ appear to remember experiences.
   a. 1 week
   b. 6 weeks
   c. 1 month
   d. 3 months

___ 4. Babies are most likely to remember photographs of
   a. the human face.
   b. abstract patterns.
   c. animals.
   d. multicolored circles.

___ 5. Mr. Mason is changing his 7-month-old son's diaper. Mr. Mason notices that Scott keeps looking at one side of the changing table and appears to be puzzled. Mr. Mason remembers that a small stuffed animal bear is usually there. Mr. Mason finds the bear and shows it to Scott. Scott's eyes brighten and he begins to move his arms and hands. The fact that Scott could remember the bear without seeing it is evidence of
   a. stimulus memory.
   b. productive memory.
   c. repitition memory.
   d. delayed memory.

___ 6. _____ came to believe that children do not necessarily think the same way adults do.
   a. Skinner
   b. Piaget
   c. Watson
   d. Chomsky

_____ 7. With _____ the subject makes a response because he is rewarded in some way.
   a. operant conditioning
   b. classical conditioning
   c. stimulus learning
   d. all of the above

_____ 8. Meltzoff has found that infants as young as 2 to 3 weeks of age have been found to imitate adult
   a. eye blinking.
   b. smiling.
   c. lip and tongue protrusions.
   d. vocalizations.

_____ 9. Researchers all agree that the infant's ability to imitate adult behaviors is the result of innate cognitive structures which enable them to acquire more information about the environment.
   a. true
   b. false

_____ 10. Identify why psychologists now believe that Piaget may have underestimated the cognitive abilities of infants.
   a. Today's innovative experimental techniques were not available to Piaget.
   b. Piaget underestimated the importance and role of perceptual learning in cognitive growth.
   c. He did not see enough infants.
   d. a & b
   e. a, b, & c

Answers to Self-Check Questions

1. c	**6.** b
2. b	**7.** a
3. c	**8.** c
4. a	**9.** b
5. b	**10.** d

CHAPTER 6

SOCIAL AND EMOTIONAL DEVELOPMENT DURING INFANCY

STUDY GOALS

After reading and studying Chapter 6, you should be able to:

1. Appreciate that the infant is a social being, born with the desire to be close to people and with capacity to interact and influence her caregivers.

2. Describe the sensory and perceptual capacities the infant possesses and how she uses them to communicate with her caregivers.

3. Discuss what is meant by the concept of *reciprocal relationship* between infant and caregiver and its importance in infant social development.

4. Describe Bowlby's theory of infant attachment and the ethnological evidence to support attachment behavior.

5. Describe how Ainsworth amplified and refined Bowlby's theory to make it more applicable to the human mother-infant relationship and empirical investigation.

6. Discuss the recent empirical evidence that supports the importance of the attachment relationship in the infant's development and the implications for subsequent development in children.

7. Define the terms *stranger anxiety* and *separation anxiety* and discuss their significance in the infant's attachment relationship and development.

8. Appreciate that there are many influences (both of infant and attachment figure) which influence the development and quality of the attachment relationship.

9. Define the term *social referencing* and understand how this ability of the infant is an important factor in how she acquires the ability to manage her own emotional expressions and states.

10. Describe how the work of Harlow, Spitz and others has provided insight into the consequences of maternal deprivation and separation in relation to the infant's development of attachment to the caregiver and subsequent development.

11. Appreciate the infant's need for consistency and continuity of care and discuss how this relates to issues of foster care, working mothers, and day care.

12. Describe the recent evidence which describes the unique aspects of the father's role in the infant's development and his relationship with the infant.

13. Appreciate that the infant is part of a larger social system and that the relationship the infant has with siblings, peers, and caregivers other than mother and father may have an impact on the infant's social development.

REVIEWING THE CHAPTER

I. Are infants social beings?
(pp. 263–281; study goals 1, 2, 3, 7, 9)

The human infant is born with greater physiological and intellectual abilities than was previously recognized. The infant is also a social being with the desire and need to be close to people. The ability of the infant to gaze, cry, cling, and smile all contribute to the infant's being able to attract people to her and maintain an interaction. Although much of the research has focused on the mother's role in the mother-infant dyad, we now recognize that the mother and infant each influence the other in what has been termed a reciprocal interaction or turn taking. Research by Stern and Brazelton points to the fact that both mother (or caregiver) and infant are gradually learning about each other's characteristics and needs and gradually modifying their behavior in accordance with the other. The *synchrony* is dependent on the following: (1) the infant's ability to signal her needs; (2) the infant's capacity to respond to her mother's behavior, and (3) the mother's ability to perceive the infant's signals and respond appropriately.

This synchrony takes time and effort to develop on the part of both the infant and mother. At times, patterns develop between mother and infant which lead to barriers and disorders in their relationship. Infants who cry continuously and who are unresponsive to the mother's overtures may be difficult to care for and may make the mother feel rejected and helpless in her ability to effectively care for the infant. Equally important is the possibility that the mother may be unresponsive or intrusive in her interactions with the infant. The infant gradually learns she is not able to make her feelings known and stops trying. Thus, the central task of infancy is for the infant to develop a sense of basic trust in her caregiver and the feeling that the world is a safe and secure place to be.

Infants have various ways of communicating their needs, which become more elaborate as they develop. Crying is the most profound way an infant can communicate with her environment. Mothers differ in their ability to ascertain why an infant is crying and their ability to comfort the infant. Although mothers frequently believe that responding to a crying baby will lead to reinforcing the crying or in spoiling the baby, research has shown that in fact the opposite is true. Infants whose mothers respond to their cries soon learn that they do not need to cry a great deal to elicit their mother's attention.

The ability of the infant to gaze at the mother is also a very important mechanism to initiate and maintain an interaction with the mother. By the time the infant is 4 to 6 weeks old, her visual motor system has developed to the extent that she can fixate on her mother's eyes. This ability to establish eye contact is an important developmental milestone which makes the mother feel as if she is caring for a real person who is interacting with her.

The infant's ability to smile has been viewed as her most social emotional expression. During the first year of life, there appear to be three stages of smiling. First is the *endogenous* or *spontaneous smile,* which seems to be the result of central nervous system activity. This smile does not signify a conscious sense of pleasure. The second stage of smiling behavior is called the *nonselective social smile* or *exogenous smile.* This smile is triggered by something in the environment, usually when watching the human face or hearing the mother's voice. The *selective social smile* is the last to emerge and reflects the infant's ability to smile at individuals she is familiar with and not to smile at unfamiliar faces. There has been a great deal of theoretical interest in infant smiles from numerous perspectives. The evolutionary theory emphasizes the adaptive value of the smile and variations that occur depending on childrearing settings. Cognitive theorists emphasize that the smile is an innate expression of pleasure that infants experience when they master a task.

Psychologists also emphasize the role that fear plays in the infant's development. Two fears, stranger anxiety and separation anxiety, are normal fears of the infant in the second half of the first year of life. These fears indicate the infant is forming attachment relationships to those adults who care for her, for the infant begins to be afraid of unfamiliar adults and exhibit distressed behavior when an adult to whom she is attached leaves.

Research has also indicated that infants are capable of using another person's behavior to form an understanding of a social situation and how to respond to it. This ability is called *social referencing.* Emotional expressions of an adult can help an infant regulate her behavior in unfamiliar and potentially dangerous situations. Thus, the infant uses the social context for understanding emotional reactions.

II. What is the significance of attachment in establishing relationships?
   (pp. 282–291; study goals 4, 5, 6, 8, 10)

Attachment is considered one of the most important of the infant's emotional experiences. It is defined as the strong and enduring bond that develops between the infant and the person he is most frequently with. Attachment does not develop instantly, but occurs in phases during the first year of life. John Bowlby was instrumental in conceptualizing attachment theory from an ethnological perspective in which the infant seeks protection from harm and has innate abilities to elicit proximity to the caregiver. Building on Bowlby's work, Mary Ainsworth developed the notion of "a secure base in which to explore" and "preferential treatment under stress" as a way of identifying the quality of mother-infant attachment. She developed the laboratory experiment, the *Strange Situation Procedure,* to assess individual differences in the attachment relationship. She was able to classify infants in terms of the security of their attachment relationship as either securely attached, anxiously attached, or avoidantly attached. An infant with a secure attachment is considered to have the healthiest pattern of attachment and subsequently has the capacity to enjoy sharing and social interactions with parents and peers in the preschool years.

There are numerous factors, from both infant and attachment figure, which influence the development and quality of the attachment process. The caregiver's responsiveness to the infant's crying and amount of interaction with the infant have been found to be related to the quality of the attachment. The mother's sensitivity and responsiveness to the infant's signals have also been shown to be factors in the development of the attachment relationship. The infant's character-istics, such as unresponsiveness and problems with physiological regulation, may influence how a mother responds to the infant and thus the establishment of the attachment relationship. Numerous lines of research have indicated that attachment is a crucial factor in many aspects of the infant's development. The infant who feels secure and has a sense of trust in his environment has been found to be more independent, competent, self-directed, and mature as a preschooler than a child who had patterns of insecure attachment as an infant.

The work of Harlow and Spitz has provided insight into what happens to the attachment relationship when there is maternal deprivation and separation. Harlow's studies with surrogate mother monkeys indicated that although infant monkey's preferred the cloth surrogate to the wire lactating surrogate for comfort, these infant monkeys displayed bizarre behavior later in life. In studying institu-tionalized infants, Spitz found that infants became depressed not from the lack of good physical care but from a lack of nurturant care or mothering. Recent work comparing two groups of infants, one group that remained in an orphanage and the other group that was adopted into a more socially responsive environment, indicates that the negative effects of early deprivation may be reversed once the infant is given appropriate care. These findings point out the importance of con-tingent and consistent care for the infant.

III. What are the social issues related to infant social development?
    (pp. 291–303; study goals 11–13)

The knowledge we have regarding the importance of a secure attachment rela-tionship and sensitive, consistent caregiving has important implications for con-siderations of working mothers, day care, and foster care. In regard to working mothers and the use of day care, the majority of studies show that infants develop emotional bonds in much the same way and at the same time as infants who are reared at home—the main bonds are to the parents not the day care provider. However, recent work indicates that infants who come from highly stressed fam-ilies that use out-of-home care that varies in quality may be vulnerable to devel-oping an insecure mother-infant attachment. The recognition of the importance of continuity and sensitive care coupled with the problem of finding high quality infant day care has led those concerned about the welfare of children and families to consider the possibility of a paid infant care leave during which parents can look after the care of their baby. The United States is one of the few industrialized nations that does not have such a policy.

Changes have also been made in the foster care system as we have begun to learn more about the importance of continuity of care for the infant and young child. These efforts include the following: (1) preventive services to help families avoid the use of foster care; (2) attempts to reunite foster children with their biological parents, and (3) permanent adoptive families for children who cannot return home.

Although fathers have always been part of families, it has been only recently that the father's role in the infant's development has been investigated. It has been found that fathers are as competent as mothers in taking care of infants and have a unique role with the infant that includes an attachment relationship and a more playful, physical relationship with the infant than the mother has. In addition, the study of infants within a broader social setting has resulted in an interest in infant-peer relations. Recent work indicates that infants are fascinated with each other and that infants follow a developmental sequence in how they relate to each other. Initially infants look at each other; at about four months they try to touch each other; and at about six months they begin to smile at each other. Once they are more mobile they begin to approach each other.

SIGNIFICANT CONCEPTS, PEOPLE, AND TOPICS

You should become familiar with and be able to explain the following concepts, people, and topics. Most of the terms are highlighted in the margins of the text and some are also defined in the glossary at the end of the text.

reciprocal relationship	*synchrony in mother-infant*
intrusive mothering	*relationship*
trust vs. mistrust	*baby talk*
infant gaze	*endogenous smile*
nonselective exogenous smile	*selective exogenous smile*
stranger anxiety	*separation anxiety*
social referencing	*attachment*
Strange Situation Procedure	*securely attached*
anxious attachment	*avoidant attachment*
behavioral system	*Harlow's studies*
consistency and continuity of care	*foster care*
infant care leave	*family system*
peer relations	*early deprivation*
Daniel Stern	*T. B. Brazelton*
John Bowlby	*Mary Ainsworth*
Michael Lamb	*Harry Harlow*
René Spitz	

50

SELF-CHECK

Choose the response that best answers the question or completes the statement.

_____ 1. The infant communicates and engages the parents' attention in the following ways:
   a. crying
   b. gazing
   c. smiling
   d. clinging
   e. a, b, c
   f. a, b, c, d

_____ 2. The baby's ability to establish eye contact is an important milestone in social development. Mothers report that they feel the baby is really looking at them for the first time when the baby is around _____ weeks old.
   a. 8
   b. 6
   c. 4
   d. 2

_____ 3. Mothers have been told that responding immediately to a crying baby will not spoil the baby. Researchers have found this to be
   a. true
   b. false

_____ 4. Maggy is an 8-month-old baby. While near her mother, she actively explores the surrounding environment, but when something frightens her, she rushes to her mother for comfort. This response is indicative of
   a. secure attachment.
   b. avoidant attachment.
   c. anxious, ambivalent attachment.
   d. close attachment.

_____ 5. Which type of infant attachment relationship is the best predictor of the occurrence of the major psychological difficulty in adulthood?
   a. avoidant attachment
   b. secure attachment
   c. ambivalent, anxious attachment
   d. none of the above

_____ 6. Infants are born with one generalized emotional reaction, which is
   a. fear.
   b. distress.
   c. delight.
   d. excitement.

_____ 7. The infant's development of smiling behavior occurs in the following sequence:
   a. nonselective exogenous, selective exogenous, endogenous.
   b. nonselective endogenous, selective endogenous, exogenous.
   c. exogenous, nonselective endogenous, selective endogenous.
   d. endogenous, nonselective exogenous, selective exogenous.

_____ 8. The consensus of childrearing experts is that parents should
      a. keep the baby on a strict schedule.
      b. respond in a way that encourages the baby's trust.
      c. allow the baby to cry so she won't become spoiled.
      d. begin toilet training by the time the baby is 1-year old.
_____ 9. Depression in infants
      a. does not occur if the infant is under 18 months of age.
      b. has been observed in situations where infants are kept clean and fed, but are given little nurturant care.
      c. has been observed in situations involving prolonged separation from the mother.
      d. b & c
      e. a, b, c
_____ 10. The infant-mother relationship can best be characterized as
      a. a reciprocal relationship between mother and infant.
      b. the infant's behavioral style influencing the mother.
      c. the mother's effect on the infant.

Answers to Self-Check Questions

1. f	**6.** d
2. c	**7.** d
3. a	**8.** b
4. a	**9.** d
5. d	**10.** a

STUDY GOALS

This is the first of four short sections that consider issues surrounding atypical development in the infant, early childhood, middle childhood, and adolescent years. After reading and studying the section on Atypical Development in Infancy, you should be able to:

1. Discuss the various points of view on how society should protect the rights of severely handicapped infants, and who should be responsible for making life-or-death decisions in their behalf.

2. List the explanations that have been offered for the rise in births of handicapped infants.

3. Explain the value of screening tests and contrast these with diagnostic tests.

4. List several factors that may place infants at risk for various conditions, and explain how these risks may be limited.

5. Describe the characteristics of developmental disabilities, such as infant blindness, congenital deafness, and cerebral palsy.

6. Name some of the goals of early intervention programs.

REVIEWING THE SECTION

The Baby Jane Doe case highlights the dilemmas presented by advances in medical technology that permit us to extend the lives of severely handicapped infants. In its decision to enter the case, the federal government raised two questions: (1) How should society protect the rights of severely handicapped infants? and (2) Who should make life-or-death decisions in their behalf? After issuing regulations prohibiting discriminatory failure to feed and care for handicapped or seriously ill infants, the federal government found itself in contention with some parents and physicians, who argue that case-by-case decisions should be made depending on the severity of the handicap and the ultimate prospects for recovery. One suggested compromise is that hospitals create infant bioethical review committees including professionals and lay people. However, it is doubtful that such groups could operate within the short timespan in which these decisions must normally be made.

There is also disagreement over whether it is medical technology that is responsible for doubling the number of handicapped infants born annually over the past quarter century. While some attribute the trend to increased cigarette smoking and exposure to other teratogens among women of child-bearing age, others trace the apparent increase to earlier detection of handicaps.

Early detection has been assisted over the past 25 years by screening tests and by the recognition that optimal development of a handicapped child depends on early identification and prompt referral. Infants at risk for various disorders are identified by screening tests, retested to confirm the original testing, and, if warranted, they are sent for formal diagnostic evaluation. Examples of factors which may place infants at risk are prenatal and perinatal complications, maternal smoking, low birth weight, postmaturity, prematurity, and prenatal malnutrition. Many of the problems associated with these risk factors may be prevented by identifying these infants and alerting parents to their babies' vulnerabilities and characteristics.

Among the disorders identified by screening tests are developmental disabilities. These are chronic disorders which can be manifest in mental or physical impairment and are likely to result in constrained ability to learn and to function independently. Examples of such disabilities include mental retardation, blindness, deafness, and cerebral palsy.

If an infant is helped to compensate for her handicap, a developmental disability such as blindness or congenital deafness may not always dampen her capacity for developmental progress. In this belief, many early intervention programs have been founded in order to prevent disorders that may arise from genetic or adverse influences on development, to remediate the effects of identified disorders, and to provide families with access to services. For instance, parents may use auditory cues to reduce the temporary delays in motor, cognitive, linguistic, and social development shown by blind infants. Similarly, early detection of congenital deafness can avert the language deficiencies that otherwise appear and gradually worsen after 9 months of age.

The breadth of individual differences among the handicapped is especially evident among those with cerebral palsy. This developmental disability stems from brain damage occurring during the prenatal or perinatal period and is characterized by some form of motor dysfunction. There are striking differences in the limitations imposed by cerebral palsy and the severity of the handicaps associated with it.

SIGNIFICANT CONCEPTS AND TOPICS

You should become familiar with and be able to explain the following concepts, terms, and topics. Most of the terms are highlighted in the margins of the text and some are also defined in the glossary at the end of the text.

atypical development

teratogenic effects

diagnosis

postmaturity

cerebral palsy

infant bioethical review committees

screening

at-risk infants

developmental disabilities

early intervention programs

SELF-CHECK

Choose the response that best answers the question or completes the statement.

_____ 1. The Baby Jane Doe case led to
   a. PL 94–142, the Education for All Handicapped Children Act.
   b. federal child care subsidies for families with handicapped children.
   c. a public debate on the role of government in protecting the rights of severely handicapped infants.
   d. all of the above

_____ 2. Congenital deafness
   a. is usually detected when an infant fails to develop babbling.
   b. often escapes detection for several months.
   c. results in irreversible setbacks in language development even when detected early.
   d. none of the above

_____ 3. Risk factors include
   a. prenatal malnutrition.
   b. low birth weight.
   c. maternal smoking.
   d. all of the above

_____ 4. The Prenatal Risk Factor Scale is an example of
   a. an early intervention program.
   b. a diagnostic test.
   c. a screening test.
   d. none of the above

_____ 5. Cerebral palsy
   a. stems from prenatal or perinatal brain damage.
   b. is always characterized by some form of mental dysfunction.
   c. usually doesn't emerge until adolescence.
   d. is a disease that attacks the muscles in childhood.

Answers to Self-Check Questions

1. c
2. b
3. d
4. c
5. a

CHAPTER 7

PHYSICAL DEVELOPMENT DURING THE PRESCHOOL YEARS

STUDY GOALS

After reading and studying Chapter 7, you should be able to:

1. Appreciate that the changes in physical growth during the preschool years facilitate the transition of the individual from baby to child.

2. Discuss the increased competence and independence of the preschool child in regard to specific self-help skills, fine and gross motor development.

3. Discuss the role that environmental influences such as nutrition, poverty, health, and emotions play in the physical and motor development of the child.

4. Describe the role that myelination of the nerve fibers in the brain plays in the developmental progression of the child in relation to accomplishment of complex gross and fine motor tasks and language ability.

5. Discuss the biological and cultural influences which contribute to gender similarities and differences in motor development and ability.

6. Appreciate that disorders such as failure-to-thrive, deprivation dwarfism, and obesity are the result of an interaction of parent, child, and environmental characteristics.

7. Discuss the factors which have contributed to the recent improved health status of children in the United States and at the same time have produced gaps in the services to children.

8. Discuss the role that poverty plays in the health and subsequent development of children.

9. Describe the factors which have contributed to both the progress and lack of progress in regard to accident prevention and its related programs and policies.

REVIEWING THE CHAPTER

I. What physical changes occur during the preschool period?
(pp. 319–327; study goals 1 and 4)

Although the physical changes are not as dramatic as during infancy, the preschool child usually gains 4 to 5 pounds a year, grows about 3 inches, and on the average at age 6 weighs 45 pounds and is 43 inches tall. Not only is the preschool child growing, but her body proportions are becoming more adult-like. There are also significant changes in skeletal maturation and brain growth, which allow the preschooler to develop a sense of competence and independence in her self-help activities and motor tasks. Thus, during this period the child learns how to skip, climb, throw objects, undress and dress herself, feed herself, become toilet trained, and acquire fine motor skills such as writing and drawing. The preschool child has increased strength due to the rapid rate of bone ossification in which the bones are becoming longer, thicker, and harder. Another important internal change that occurs during the preschool years is growth and maturation of the brain. The increase in brain weight is due to the increase in the size of neurons. This reflects the fact that a myelination cycle is occurring in several functional areas of the brain. This myelination process is associated with the child gaining increased language ability and control of fine motor skills. During these years the brain becomes increasingly organized into two hemispheres: the right hemisphere codes images and the left hemisphere codes linguistic descriptions.

II. What does the preschool child learn to master?
(pp. 328–336; study goals 2 and 5)

The preschool child develops a proficiency in both gross and fine motor skills, much of which happens in the context of the child's play. Due to the gradual process of brain maturation, the preschooler attains mastery of gross motor tasks before competence in fine motor tasks is attained. Thus, we see the 3-year-old child attempting to master the gross motor skills of running, jumping, climbing, and the 6-year-old child attempting to master fine motor skills such as writing, drawing, dressing, and tying his shoes. Gender differences in motor development and proficiency are due to differences in boys' and girls' motor development and cultural expectations. Differences in muscles, bone growth and ossification, and body fat result in boys usually being superior in gross motor skills and girls better in fine motor skills. However, physical differences between boys and girls alone cannot account for the variations in mastery of certain skills.

Cultural expectations of appropriate behavior encourage children to develop in certain sex-role defined ways. Toilet training is a major accomplishment for the preschool child. Although most children are trained by the time they are 3 years old, there are individual differences due to differences in muscle maturation and parental and societal expectations. Although in some societies toilet training is accomplished by the time the child is 1 year old, currently our culture seems to accept a more child oriented approach in which the process is not even initiated until the child is at least 18 months old.

III. What are the factors which influence the preschooler's growth?
(pp. 336–340; study goals 3 and 6)

Although genetic differences account for variations in the rate of a child's growth, environmental influences such as nutrition, health care, and emotional factors contribute significantly to the child's growth and development. It is known that malnutrition has far reaching effects on the developing child's physical and cognitive capacities. Malnutrition can result from dietary malnourishment, but more recently it has been determined that children can suffer from emotional malnutrition. This occurs when children are in a highly stressed caregiving arrangement such as with a socially unresponsive caregiver. Failure-to-thrive and deprivation dwarfism in young children have been related to mothering disorders. However, recent evidence indicates that the relationship between maternal attitudes and child behaviors is very complex and that there are characteristics of the child which contribute to this maladaptive outcome. Although obesity is not usually considered a problem with preschoolers, recent evidence indicates it deserves more attention. Overweight children are likely to grow up to be overweight or obese adolescents and adults. During the preschool period, the child is vulnerable to many infections and illnesses. However, due to the increase in preventive health care and immunizations for preschoolers, the health of these children has improved dramatically over the past two decades.

IV. What are the social issues which influence child health care?
(pp. 340–347; study goals 7, 8, 9)

Although the availability of health care for children has improved, there are still problems which compromise children's health. The most influential factor is poverty. One out of every five children grows up in poverty. These children are exposed to chronic malnutrition and poor health, which have been linked to problems in motivation and achievement and the increased incidence of behavior problems and delinquency. Although Medicaid provides health care to needy children, there are financial barriers and varying state guidelines that compromise its efficacy. Preventive health services for young children have been shown to be instrumental in reducing visual and hearing deficits. These services not only positively influence learning and language development, they also are cost effective. However, in times of fiscal restraint, health services for children are often the first items cut from the budget. Accident prevention has been of interest to policy makers in the United States due to the large number of children that are victims of accidents and the belief that most accidents are preventable. To date, accident policy and programs have had limited effectiveness due to a lack of recognition of the multiple causes and concerns which need to be addressed. Safety measures need to go beyond parent education to include policies that could be mandated by law. The problem is one of balancing the safety needs of children with the freedom of the individual.

SIGNIFICANT CONCEPTS, TERMS, AND TOPICS

You should become familiar with and be able to explain the following concepts, terms, and topics. Most of the terms are highlighted in the margins of the text and some are also defined in the glossary at the end of the text.

skeletal maturity   *glial cells*
myelination   *myelogenetic cycles*
right hemisphere   *left hemisphere*
linguistic descriptions   *images*
plasticity of the brain   *bone age*
gross motor skills   *fine motor skills*
self-help skills   *malnutrition*
failure to thrive   *obesity*
new morbidity   *Medicaid*
preventive health care

SELF-CHECK

Choose the response that best answers the question or completes the statement.

_____ 1. Between the ages of 2 and 6, the child usually gains _____ and grows _____ each year.
   a. 2 pounds; 3 inches
   b. 3 pounds; 4 inches
   c. 4–5 pounds; 3 inches
   d. none of the above

_____ 2. In the preschool period, the child's development of motor skills serves the function of
   a. becoming proficient in performing complex motor tasks.
   b. learning self-help skills.
   c. allowing the child to become more independent.
   d. b and c
   e. all of the above

_____ 3. As a psychologist, you are talking to a group of parents about children in the preschool period. You tell them that the preschool child usually masters all but one of the following developmental tasks. Select the one the child usually _does not_ master.
   a. dressing herself
   b. tying her shoes
   c. toilet training
   d. printing her name with a pencil
   e. cutting her food with a fork and knife

_____ 4. Jane, a 6-year-old, is very short for her age. The pediatrician recommends that an x-ray of her hand be taken to determine bone age. The results of the x-ray indicate that she has the bone age of a 4-year-old. This means that her eventual height would be
   a. unable to be determined from an x-ray of the hand.
   b. taller than normal.
   c. within normal limits.
   d. shorter than normal.

_____ 5. By the time a child is 5 years old, the brain has attained _____ percent of its adult weight.
   a. 90
   b. 95
   c. 70
   d. none of the above

_____ 6. _____ accidents are the leading cause of fatalities in children from 1 to 4 years of age.
   a. Poisoning
   b. Choking
   c. Drowning
   d. Car

_____ 7. The preschool child is able to undress herself before she is able to dress herself.
   a. true
   b. false
_____ 8. The single most influential factor affecting the health status of children is
   a. chronic illness.
   b. family predisposition for illnesses.
   c. premature birth of the child.
   d. poverty.
_____ 9. The new morbidity for health problems in children refers to
   a. accidents.
   b. child abuse.
   c. learning problems.
   d. a and b
   e. all of the above
_____ 10. Malnutrition during the preschool years can have deleterious effects on the child's
   a. resistance to infectious disease.
   b. social responsiveness.
   c. intellectual abilities.
   d. a and c
   e. all of the above

Answers to Self-Check Questions

1. c	**6.** d
2. e	**7.** a
3. e	**8.** d
4. c	**9.** d
5. a	**10.** e

CHAPTER 8

COGNITIVE AND LANGUAGE DEVELOPMENT
DURING THE PRESCHOOL YEARS

STUDY GOALS

After reading and studying Chapter 8, you should be able to:

1. List the characteristics of Piaget's preoperational stage of cognitive development.

2. Discuss the development and significance of symbolic functioning in the preschool years.

3. Contrast symbols and signs.

4. Explain the importance of conceptual development and its relationship to classification skills and to performance on the part-whole problem in the preschool period.

5. Relate the notions of irreversibility and centering to the preschooler's performance on conservation tasks.

6. Describe the evidence that preschool children are less egocentric than Piaget claimed.

7. Describe the major elements of language development between the ages of 2 and 6, including changes in sentence length, use of negation, question formation, articulation, and grammatical rule use.

8. Contrast egocentric and socialized speech, and summarize current evidence against Piaget's contention that a pattern of egocentric speech persists until about age 7.

9. Contrast the positions of Piaget and Vygotsky regarding the relationship between language and thought.

10. Describe how parents can enhance children's cognitive growth, optimize their chances for success in school, and encourage positive attitudes toward learning.

11. List some characteristics of a well-run day care center and summarize the evidence regarding the relationship between developmental progress and day care (vs. home care).

12. Explain how parents can enhance the benefits of the preschool child's exposure to television.

13. Describe the goals and characteristics of nursery school programs and contrast these with day care programs.

14. Briefly describe what has been learned from evaluations of preschool intervention programs, including those in Project Head Start.

REVIEWING THE CHAPTER

I. How does thought change during the preschool years?
    (pp. 350–367; study goals 1 to 6)

Between the second year of life and age 6 or 7, the child is in what Piaget called the *preoperational period* of cognitive development, which is distinguished from the preceding sensorimotor period by major changes in *symbolic functioning*. The child can now understand, create, and use symbols to represent things which are not present and he gradually makes the transition from symbols to *signs,* which have public meanings that are shared and understood by society. *Symbolic play* and *deferred imitation* are additional manifestations of these changes in symbolic functioning. It is through symbolic play, Piaget argued, that the child acquires the meanings of things by assimilating them into his mental construction of the world. For this reason, Piaget contended that it was important not to hurry the child through this stage of make-believe. Others note that the preschooler's imaginative play may be, in essence, the creativity and individuality that we value in older children and adults.

Concept development—progress in the ability to generalize what is known about a specific object or event to other similar objects and events—is another important characteristic of preoperational thought. In addition to its role in simplifying learning by allowing us to extend our knowledge of one object to a class of similar objects, concept development is instrumental to the refinement of classification skills. Although Piaget argued that it is not until the end of the preoperational period, around age 6 or 7, that children acquire the ability to classify objects simultaneously along several dimensions, much research suggests that children acquire classification skills well before this point, perhaps as early as age 4. Nonetheless, even children who can classify objects have difficulty with *part-whole* problems that require an understanding of the hierarchical relationships among categories.

Preschoolers show equally poor performance on *conservation tasks* and are easily fooled by appearances. Piaget attributed these difficulties to the *irreversibility* of preschoolers' thought and to their tendency to *center* on one dimension of a problem while ignoring others.

The preoperational child uses a special brand of logic. He tends to use neither the inductive nor the deductive reasoning familiar to adults, but *transductive rea-*

soning, going from one particular to the next and ascribing cause and effect status to unrelated events. Piaget argues that such beliefs as *finalism, artificialism,* and *animism* may stem from the child's use of this logic to assimilate reality to his own schema.

According to Piagetian theory, *egocentrism* is another characteristic of pre-operational children. His major piece of evidence for this belief was the apparent inability of children under 9 to accurately identify the views of a display that others who were positioned differently would see. However, experiments simplifying this task by changing the mode of response or the form of the problem indicate that children as young as 4 years are able to give the correct answers.

Today, developmental psychologists have moved from a largely negative picture of preschool cognitive development to concentrate on the competencies of these children. Many researchers have also developed alternative, information processing accounts of cognitive development.

II. How does language acquisition proceed in the preschool years?
(pp. 367–375; study goals 7 to 9)

Toward the end of the second year, the child begins to combine words and, thereafter, his sentences gradually lengthen, his vocabulary increases rapidly, and his articulation improves. However, perhaps because the young child is egocentric in his thinking, he may make up words and expect others to understand him or define words in terms of actions that *he* performs. In addition, some words, such as those that convey comparison, are difficult for preschoolers to use appropriately.

Nevertheless, preschoolers don't just learn words; they acquire the rules of grammar in a remarkably regular order. For instance, the child first indicates questions only by intonation, then by placing a question word at the beginning of a sentence without further modification, and finally, by applying a specific rule—placing the verb before the subject. Similarly, the child comes to show correct use of negation, though initially he may simply say *no* at the start of a sentence. The most powerful evidence that children acquire grammatical rules is that they often *overregularize* their speech by changing irregular words and grammatical exceptions to conform to the rules.

The functions of speech also change as children get older. Piaget contended that children move from *collective monologues* and largely *egocentric speech* at the beginning of the preschool period to *socialized speech,* which seeks to exchange information with a listener. Current research suggests that egocentric speech does not last as long as Piaget had thought; preschoolers do seem to listen and respond to each other's statements and even 4-year-olds modify their speech for younger listeners. Nonetheless, they often overestimate the clarity of their messages.

Another major debate concerns the question, "Do children first have a thought and then try to express it in words or does language shape their thoughts?" Piaget felt that language was only possible via the development of cognition and could be viewed as a vehicle for expressing thought. However, theorists such as Lev Vygotsky have assigned language a more significant role. Vygotsky contended that with the beginning of symbolic thinking at about age 2, language comes to regulate the child's thoughts and behavior through egocentric speech. Whereas Piaget argued that egocentric speech declines and disappears, Vygotsky contended that it is gradually internalized. Others, such as Lois Bloom and Jerome Bruner, see language as a tool provided by culture that expands the child's capacity to learn.

III. What are the contexts in which preschoolers develop and how can they be improved?
(pp. 375–390; study goals 10–14)

Between 2 and 6, the child's home is his primary learning environment. Here, parents may enhance their preschooler's intellectual competence by providing safe surroundings that engender security, supporting the child's tendency toward autonomy, offering freedom to explore the world and to express feelings, challenging the child to master the developmental tasks he confronts, and providing him with assistance as he needs it. Parents may also enhance a child's benefit from television exposure by watching with him, guiding him toward appropriate programming, and being ready to explain what he sees. This sort of mediation is important, because young children often have difficulty interpreting the relationship between camera shots and understanding the visual signals used on television. Direct access to television, without parental intervention, is now easier to obtain and researchers note that particularly heavy viewers may lag behind their peers in intellectual development.

Since the number of preschoolers in some form of day care has quadrupled over the past two decades and is expected to increase even further, this is another context in which a great deal of preschoolers' development takes place. In general, research suggests that children in a well-run day care center are at no developmental disadvantage when compared to children who spend most of their time at home. Moreover, a good day care center is likely to provide more educational opportunities than some children would encounter at home. However, the quality of a day care center is not determined by the availability of academic training, but by the behaviors and attitudes of caretakers toward the children, the presence of sufficient numbers of caregivers, maintenance of class sizes under 13 for 3-year-olds and under 16 for older children, and the provision of safe surroundings and a variety of play materials. A close relationship between parents and caregivers, though currently atypical, has been shown by Head Start experience to benefit both parents and children and to facilitate caregivers' ability to relate appropriately to the children.

Children not enrolled in day care often take part in a preschool program several mornings a week, which gives them an opportunity to learn to get along with peers and with an adult in a position of authority. Preschools also offer opportunities to play with materials not available at home, to develop cognitive skills, and to become familiar with a school routine. Though day care programs may incorporate many of the features of nursery schools, nursery schools do not care for children for long periods of time.

66

Such preschool programs were an important part of an effort begun in the 1960s to enhance the development of disadvantaged children. On the theory that the cycle of poverty could be interrupted and equal opportunity enhanced by the provision of early supplementary education, *Project Head Start* was made a part of the War on Poverty. Comprising over 2000 programs for enhancing the quality of life of children and families, Head Start varies in its characteristics from site to site. This variation results partly from the choice to adopt a culturally relativistic approach that respects children's varied backgrounds and emphasizes the involvement of parents in planning and administration of each program. This involvement, in turn, has led parents to feel better about themselves and their children to feel that they have more control over their lives and to be more motivated to achieve in school.

The earlier evaluations of Head Start created false optimism, since initial IQ gains appeared to fade out as children got older. However, later research on preschool interventions recognized the error in concentrating so heavily on IQ. These studies found that Head Start improved children's health and feelings about themselves, both of which affect academic performance. Evaluations have also documented the *cost-effectiveness* of preschool interventions.

SIGNIFICANT CONCEPTS, PEOPLE, AND TOPICS

You should become familiar with and be able to explain the following concepts, people, and topics. Most of the terms are highlighted in the margins of the text and some are also defined in the glossary at the end of the text.

Jean Piaget

preoperational period

symbolic functioning

symbolic play

symbols

concepts

class inclusion

part-whole problem

irreversibility

centering

deductive reasoning

finalism

animism

perspective-taking

information processing

Roger Brown

morphemes

sensorimotor period

representational thought

deferred imitation

signs

prelogical thinking

classification

Piagetian tasks

conservation

transformation

inductive reasoning

transductive reasoning

artificialism

egocentrism

three mountain task

telegraphic speech

grammatical rules

overregulation

67

articulation
socialized speech
Lev Vygotsky
National Day Care Study
Child Development Associate
Maria Montessori
Project Head Start
cost-effectiveness

egocentric speech
collective monologue
day care
staff-child ratio
nursery school
War on Poverty
program evaluation

SELF-CHECK

Choose the response that best answers the question or completes the statement.

____ 1. The preoperational child
   a. does not exhibit deferred imitation.
   b. can use symbols to represent things which are not present.
   c. has not yet achieved the milestones of the sensorimotor period.
   d. demonstrates an understanding of conservation and the reversibility of transformations.

____ 2. Unlike symbols, signs
   a. are used very early in the preoperations period.
   b. are neologisms often understandable only to the user.
   c. have public meanings easily understood by others.
   d. are widely used only by egocentric children.

____ 3. Janet, 4, watches as water is poured from a short, wide container into a tall, thin one. She is then asked whether there is as much water in the tall, thin container as there had been in the short, wide one. She responds that there is more water in the tall container because it goes up higher. Her response is an example of
   a. transductive reasoning.
   b. deductive reasoning.
   c. reversibility.
   d. centering.

____ 4. Piaget's claim that preschool children are egocentric is disputed by evidence showing that they
   a. are able to correctly identify a photograph of the three mountain apparatus as it is seen by a person in a different position.
   b. do not assume that a blindfolded companion will have knowledge of their toy choices.
   c. can respond correctly to part-whole problems when their wording is simplified.
   d. do not modify their speech when talking to infants.

____ 5. Which of the following is offered as evidence that language development is a process of acquiring rules rather than learning words?
   a. rapid vocabulary growth
   b. overregularization
   c. the transition from symbols to signs
   d. all of the above

____ 6. Which of the following theorists is most closely identified with the view that language is primarily a vehicle for expressing thought rather than a shaper of thought?
   a. Jean Piaget
   b. Jerome Bruner
   c. Lois Bloom
   d. Lev Vygotsky

_____ 7. Which of the following is the most accurate summary of current research on the relationship between developmental progress and day care?
  a. Preschoolers who spend at least 20 hours per week in well-run day care centers *surpass* the rates of developmental progress among those in home care.
  b. Children in well-run day care centers are at no developmental disadvantage when compared to children who spend most of their time at home.
  c. Preschoolers who spend at least 20 hours per week in even a well-run day care center lag behind their peers in home care on developmental assessments.
  d. The day care center characteristics that have thus far been studied have not been linked to the developmental status of enrollees.

_____ 8. *Unlike* nursery schools, day care programs
  a. provide elementary academic training, such as instruction in the alphabet and color naming.
  b. care for children for long periods of time.
  c. are designed to prepare children for more formal schooling.
  d. all of the above

_____ 9. Complete the following sentence: As part of _____ , Project Head Start attempted to _____ by _____
  a. the New Deal; interrupt the cycle of poverty; giving supplementary grants to schools with high proportions of students on public assistance.
  b. the War on Poverty; increase equal opportunity; giving supplementary education to disadvantaged preschoolers.
  c. the War on Poverty; decrease welfare expenditures; giving supplementary grants to preschools who hired the long-term unemployed.
  d. the War on Poverty; decrease the federal budget deficit; giving job training to the chronically unemployed.

_____ 10. *Conservation* refers to
  a. the recognition that certain properties of objects are unchanged by selected transformations.
  b. the ability to use words appropriately.
  c. the ability demonstrated by correct performance on the part-whole problem.
  d. none of the above

Answers to Self-Check Questions

1. b	**6.** a
2. c	**7.** b
3. d	**8.** b
4. b	**9.** b
5. b	**10.** a

CHAPTER 9

SOCIAL AND EMOTIONAL DEVELOPMENT
DURING THE PRESCHOOL YEARS

STUDY GOALS

After reading and studying Chapter 9, you should be able to:

1. Appreciate that during the preschool period there are numerous changes in social and emotional development, which culminate in a child's increased independence and mastery of the environment.

2. Discuss the characteristics and changes in the preschool child's relationship with both mother and father.

3. Describe the impact of divorce on the preschool child.

4. Know the role that friends and friendship play in the preschool child's social and personality development.

5. Describe the developmental functions of play and the types of play behaviors that the preschool child engages in.

6. Appreciate that individual differences in a child's personality are dependent on a complex interplay of heredity and environment.

7. Discuss the developmental changes that occur in the preschool child's expression of aggression and prosocial behavior.

8. Describe how the preschool child forges a self-concept and the role that gender plays in this process.

9. Summarize how biological, environmental, and parental influences interact and influence the development of sex differences in behavior.

10. Identify and describe the three theoretical approaches that serve to explain children's acquisition of sex roles.

11. Discuss the goals of the socialization process in the preschool child.

12. Describe Baumrind's research on parenting styles and how each differently influences the child's personality characteristics.

13. Summarize what the field knows about the influence of television on the preschool child's development of aggressive and prosocial behaviors.

14. Discuss the conflicting findings in regard to the influence of day care on the preschool child's social and emotional development.

REVIEWING THE CHAPTER

I. Who is a part of the preschool child's social world?
    (pp. 394–410; study goals 1–5)

The changes in the child's social world occur against the background of the increased independence and the numerous developmental strides that characterize the preschool period. Having established a trusting relationship with her parents during infancy, the preschooler now feels secure in enjoying the company of others, meeting new people, and exploring the environment. Although the preschool child has become increasingly independent, her relationship with her parents remains the primary focus of her interactions, and her attachment to her mother continues to be strong. As mothers relax their involvement, fathers come to play a more prominent role in the child's life at this age. Fathers become increasingly involved in childrearing and spend more time playing with and disciplining the child. In addition, children, especially boys, seem to prefer their fathers to their mothers as a playmate.

Unfortunately ⅕ of children under 5 in the United States are living in single-parent homes as a result of divorce. As a consequence of divorce, there is a change in the child's relationship with both parents. The absence of the father may mean a loss of an effective disciplinarian, a role model, and emotional support. During the first year after a divorce, fathers become emotionally detached from their children and fewer than half of divorced fathers see their children even once a week. Research indicates that preschool children experience a great deal of stress at the divorce of their parents. The egocentrism of the preschool child causes him to take the blame for the divorce, feeling rejected, abandoned, and unloved. The child's adjustment is greatly influenced by the parents' post-divorce relationship.

The preschool child also has to learn to interact with and get along with younger and older siblings. The sibling relationship does include rivalry and frequent acts of confrontation and aggression. However, it has been found that the preschool child demonstrates affectionate and prosocial behaviors in sibling interactions.

The child's interest in and involvement with other children are expanding and changing during the preschool period. She has a preference for playing with children of the same sex and age; having a friend is very important. The preschool child focuses on the physical attributes of the friend rather than psychological attributes. Peer relations serve the functions of providing emotional support and learning certain social skills. Children's interactions largely take place within the context of play. During this period the child engages in four types of play behaviors: solitary play, parallel play, associate play, and cooperative play. As children get older they become more sociable in their play. By age 4 or 5, children engage in sociodramatic play—make believe play about social situations. This type of play is important for the child's development for it provides the opportunity to rehearse adult roles and understand events they experience in real life.

II. What are the issues in the preschooler's personality development?
(pp. 411–425; study goals 6–10)

The child's personality is dependent upon a complex interplay between heredity and environment. Aggression is one personality characteristic that is evident in the preschooler. Numerous theories of aggression (psychoanalytic, learning, and performance theories) differ in the degree to which they emphasize biological or psychological determinants. However, recent researchers stress the fact that both biological and environmental factors play a role in shaping the development of aggression. In spite of the preschoolers' egocentrism, these children are also capable of altruistic and prosocial behaviors in their relationships with others. The preschool child is able to show empathy and recognize when people feel happy or sad. As the child learns about other people's feelings, she is also forming her own self concept. The preschooler thinks of herself in very specific and concrete terms yet she is aware of her sense of identity and separateness.

A major task of the preschool period is the formation of gender identity and the acceptance of gender roles. By age 2½, a child is able to identify her own gender, but does not yet accept the stability or constancy of gender. This does not happen until the child is at least 5 years old. The ability of the child to accept an appropriate gender role is an important aspect of development for it organizes the child's behaviors and attitudes toward the self and others. It also influences the kinds of activities and occupations one will engage in both as a child and as an adult. Preschoolers tend to be rigid in their sex-typed behaviors and activities; however as they grow older they become more flexible. There has been a great deal of theoretical and empirical attention given to explaining sex differences in behavior. The question is whether behavioral differences between the sexes are biologically determined or learned. Psychoanalytic theory contends that identification is the basis for the sex differences whereas learning theory stresses reinforcement and punishment. The cognitive-developmental theory emphasizes a cognitive, stage model to imitation. Psychologists have found a biological basis to greater aggressiveness in males. However, experience and childrearing practices appear to account for most of the sex differences that are reported. A series of studies by Money indicates that rearing practices play a critical role in the development of gender identity and gender roles in the first three years of life. In spite of the numerous changes in our society, it is still found that parents treat sons and daughters differently and have different expectations for them which promote sex-stereotypical functioning. Research on the role of fathers indicates that the preschool period may be critical for boys' sex-role development, but not so for girls'.

III. What influences the preschool child's socialization?
(pp. 426–438; study goals 11–14)

The process by which a child comes to behave in socially acceptable ways and becomes a functioning member of society is called *socialization*. Although the family is the primary source for socialization, there are variations depending on the family characteristics such as socioeconomic status, ethnic group, and religion. The main attributes of socialization for the preschooler are self-control and social judgment. In addition, the child needs to adopt prosocial behaviors such as sharing, cooperating, and helping.

A series of studies on parenting syles by Baumrind not only found that parents differ in their approach to childrearing, but parenting practices are a major influence on the child's development. Baumrind identified three broad types of parents: authoritarian, permissive, and authoritative. Children of authoritarian parents tended to be moody, apprehensive, easily annoyed, hostile, and vulnerable to stress. Permissively reared children seemed cheerful, yet they appeared to have no self-reliance, were frequently out of control and had trouble inhibiting their impulses. The most effective and nurturant were the authoritative parents. Children of these parents tended to be the most socially competent. They were energetic, competent, cheerful, friendly, and able to approach stressful situations with curiosity. Research indicates that in order for parents to be effective in their discipline or punishment, they need to use techniques which include appropriate timing, consistency, and reason.

An extreme form of parental punishment unfortunately can result in the child being subjected to child abuse. The abusive treatment of children by their parents is a difficult social problem to understand, yet one that is receiving more societal and professional attention. Researchers are just beginning to understand the causes of child abuse, noting that it is determined by multiple forces within the individual, family, community, and culture. There is contradictory evidence as to whether adults who were subjected to abuse during their childhood years are more likely than others to be abusive parents. Factors which tend to increase the likelihood of abusive behaviors on the part of the parent are: unrealistic expectations of children, ineffective child management techniques, family stress, unemployment, large family size, overcrowded housing, alcohol abuse, and legal problems. In addition, parents are more likely to abuse children who are low-birth-weight babies or who have behavioral problems such as mental retardation or hyperactivity. Solution to the problem requires a multidisciplinary approach that includes support groups, support services for the family, and parent education programs. The consequences of abuse include neurological and physical handicaps as well as disturbances in the child's emotional and social development.

Television is a real presence in children's lives and can be viewed as an informal type of learning. Research indicates that exposure to violence on television increases a preschool child's subsequent aggression. It has also been determined that when preschool children watch television programs that attempt to teach prosocial behaviors, there is an increase in the amount of sharing, helping, and cooperative behavior they exhibit towards one another.

Day care and nursery schools are another influence on the preschool child's socialization. In such settings children have the opportunity to learn to be cooperative, helpful, wait their turn, and conform to rules. Children in full-time day care have been found to be more cooperative in their peer interactions than children who are raised at home. It has also been found that preschoolers who have been in day care since infancy are more aggressive and hostile toward peers and have more difficulty in interacting with adults than children who enter day care at age three or four. More studies are needed on the effects of day care on children's social development.

SIGNIFICANT CONCEPTS, TERMS, AND TOPICS

You should become familiar with and be able to explain the following concepts, terms, and topics. Most of the terms are highlighted in the margins of the text and some are also defined in the glossary at the end of the text.

single-parent family
sibling rivalry
parallel play
cooperative play
instrumental aggression
altruistic behavior
self-concept
gender role
reciprocal role learning
Oedipus conflict
reinforcement and punishment
self-control
prosocial behavior
authoritative parents
acts of commission
shaken baby syndrome

child support
solitary play
associative play
sociodramatic play
hostile aggression
empathy
gender identity
sex-typed behaviors
identification
Electra conflict
socialization
social judgment
authoritarian parents
permissive parents
acts of omission

SELF-CHECK

Choose the response that best answers the question or completes the statement.

_____ 1. The preschool child can be characterized as
   a. beginning to establish relationships with people other than her parents.
   b. willing to do what her parents want her to do without a fuss.
   c. enthusiastic about finding out about her environment.
   d. a & c
   e. a, b, & c

_____ 2. During the preschool period
   a. a mother is as involved with her child as she was when the child was an infant.
   b. a father begins to play a more prominent role with his child.
   c. parents begin to equally share and be involved with their child.
   d. none of the above

_____ 3. During the preschool period, boys tend to prefer to play with their
   a. grandparents.
   b. mother.
   c. father.
   d. siblings.

_____ 4. Paul is 5 years old and about to begin school. As his teacher, you identify the qualities that you expect would characterize the developmental strides Paul has made during the preschool period.
   a. Paul is able to print his name and use scissors.
   b. Paul is unable to communicate his feelings.
   c. Paul is comfortable meeting new children and developing friendships.
   d. a & b
   e. a & c
   f. a, b, & c

_____ 5. Current statistics indicate that _____ % of children under 5 years reside in single-parent families.
   a. 20
   b. 10
   c. 30
   d. 5

_____ 6. Identify which statement is *not true* of preschool children who have experienced a divorce.
   a. They experience a great deal of stress.
   b. They believe that their father is no longer part of the family.
   c. The child's egocentrism causes him to take blame for the divorce.
   d. None; all are true.

_____ 7. The preschooler's relationship with an older brother or sister can be characterized as
   a. including aggressive behavior.
   b. cooperative.
   c. affectionate.
   d. b & c
   e. a, b, & c
_____ 8. Peter, a 4-year-old boy, says to his friend Jesse, "My picture is better than yours." According to Rubin, such utterances suggest the preschool child is
   a. very competitive.
   b. learning about himself by comparing himself to others.
   c. is trying to see if he can make Jesse angry.
   d. all of the above
_____ 9. A preschooler's relationship with her friends is _____ her relationship with her parents.
   a. more egalitarian than
   b. less egalitarian than
   c. very similar to
_____ 10. _____ believed that aggression is a biological instinct that is influenced by environmental factors.
   a. Bandura
   b. Freud
   c. Lorenz
   d. Patterson

Answers to Self-Check Questions

1. d	**6.** d
2. b	**7.** e
3. c	**8.** b
4. e	**9.** a
5. a	**10.** b

ATYPICAL DEVELOPMENT IN THE EARLY CHILDHOOD YEARS

STUDY GOALS

After reading and studying the section on Atypical Development in the Early Childhood Years, you should be able to:

1. Describe how the social, linguistic, and behavioral development of autistic children differs from that of other children.

2. Discuss the mental functioning of autistic children.

3. Specify the difficulty in identifying autism and list some signs of autism that parents may notice in infancy.

4. Summarize the arguments for a biological or a genetic explanation of autism and explain why environmental accounts linking the disorder to parental characteristics have been rejected.

5. Describe current and past treatments for autism, explaining why play therapy is no longer a popular method.

REVIEWING THE SECTION

During early childhood, most children begin to establish increasingly sophisticated motor and language skills as well as their first meaningful social relationships with non-family members. However, autistic children do not fit this pattern of enjoyment of a wider social world.

Autism, which occurs in about 1 of every 2,500 children, was first identified over 40 years ago by Leo Kanner. It is characterized by several symptoms, including an inability to establish emotional and social relationships, unresponsiveness to the social environment, and avoidance of or disinterest in others. In addition, autistic children fail to acquire normal language skills. Some are functionally mute and others develop bizarre and noncommunicative speech, such as echolalia—a tendency to repeat others' words. These children do not tend to show prelinguistic skills such as babbling, but may suddenly use complete words or phrases, which they do not repeat for several months. Their behavior tends to be rigid and stereotypic, including ritual finger movements, aimless waving or ignoring of toys, rocking, head banging, self-abuse, and fixations with mechanical devices. Autistic children are resistant to change in the environment and often have unrealistic fears of common objects.

Since autistic children were once considered untestable, it has only recently been discovered that perhaps over half are also mentally retarded, with IQ scores under 50. However, some have unusual talents, which have contributed to the belief that autistics' mental functioning is normal.

Though autism may go undiagnosed for some time because autistic children are normal in their physical and motor development, some signs may be noticed by parents in the first three or four months of life. These include failure to make eye contact, rigidity when being held, and a lack of interest in adult caretakers. The autistic infant may also spend inordinate amounts of time staring at his fingers or banging his head against the crib. The deviation from normal development is usually unmistakable by 18 to 24 months of age.

Various explanations have been offered for the autistic syndrome, but researchers do not yet agree on a cause. An early theory considered autism to be emotional or social withdrawal caused by environmental factors such as unpleasurable interactions with parents. However, researchers rejected this explanation for a biological account when empirical studies failed to establish a connection between parental characteristics and childhood autism. The biological explanations of autism concentrate on brain dysfunctions that result in a child's inability to comprehend sound or make sense of what is being said. Evidence implicating organic damage as a cause of the disorder includes studies finding that more than 25% of autistic children develop seizures during late infancy. The condition has also been linked to maternal rubella during pregnancy and to metabolic disorders, such as Celiac's disease. In addition, some research points to a genetic factor. For instance, the disorder is at least three times more common in boys than in girls and there exist families in which the autistic child's siblings also show developmental disabilities, which suggests a genetic contribution. This and other factors may act singly or in combination to produce the autistic syndrome.

Treatment for autism has changed as knowledge about the disorder has increased. In the past, when autism was considered a form of emotional withdrawal, it was treated with play therapy, which was intended to help the child develop more trust in interpersonal interactions. Today, treatment focuses on helping the child acquire language skills and basic self-help skills through behavior modification techniques. Though the effectiveness of this treatment is still being studied and no current treatment produces a cure for the disorder, therapists now recognize the need to develop comprehensive programs for children and their families.

SIGNIFICANT CONCEPTS, PEOPLE, AND TOPICS

You should become familiar with and be able to explain the following concepts, people, and topics. Most of the terms are highlighted in the margins of the text and some are also defined in the glossary at the end of the text.

autism

echolalia

play therapy

Celiac's disease

Leo Kanner

Bruno Bettleheim

behavior modification techniques

SELF-CHECK

Choose the response that best answers the question or completes the statement.
____ 1. Which of the following is *not* believed to be related to autism?
   a. parental characterisitcs, such as distance and reserve
   b. metabolic disorders, such as Celiac's disease
   c. maternal rubella
   d. brain dysfunction that disturbs the comprehension of speech
____ 2. Autism often goes undiagnosed for several months because autistic children are normal in their
   a. behavioral development.
   b. social development.
   c. physical and motor development.
   d. all of the above
____ 3. Treatment of autism currently emphasizes
   a. play therapy.
   b. reintegration therapy.
   c. psychodynamic approaches.
   d. behavior modification techniques.
____ 4. The majority of autistic children
   a. are also mentally retarded.
   b. are intellectually gifted.
   c. were once the victims of child abuse.
   d. have extensive physical handicaps.
____ 5. Compared to most other children, autistic children
   a. tend to have colder and more distant parents.
   b. tend to show radically slower physical development.
   c. tend to have higher IQs.
   d. tend to show much less interest in other people.
____ 6. Environmental accounts linking autism to parental characteristics
   a. are currently preferred to biological accounts because empirical studies have found links between parental characteristics and childhood autism.
   b. have been rejected because empirical studies have failed to find links between parental characteristics and childhood autism.
   c. have not been rejected on an empirical basis, but have become unfashionable.
   d. are currently preferred to biological accounts because they provide a better explanation of the high incidence of seizures in autistic infants.

Answers to Self-Check Questions

1. a	**4.** a
2. c	**5.** d
3. d	**6.** b

CHAPTER 10

PHYSICAL DEVELOPMENT DURING MIDDLE CHILDHOOD

STUDY GOALS

After reading and studying Chapter 10, you should be able to:

1. Describe middle childhood and list some of the changes that occur during this period.

2. Describe the pace and significance of improvements in fine and gross motor skills during middle childhood.

3. Discuss the relative importance of sex, age, opportunity, personality, and genetic factors in affecting the mastery of motor skills in middle childhood.

4. List the physical changes that occur during middle childhood and describe how growth in this period compares with the pace of growth in other age periods.

5. Describe both the hypoactive and hyperactive forms of attention deficit disorder (ADD), list some of the potential causes and suggested treatments of ADD, and explain the benefits and disadvantages of treatment with stimulants.

6. Describe the secular trends in maturation and stature during middle childhood and give some potential explanations for these trends.

7. List some of the causes suggested for the recent rise in teen and preteen pregnancy, explain why this trend is harmful, discuss what can be done about it, and describe the obstacles that preventive measures have encountered.

8. Describe the three body types (endomorphic, mesomorphic, and ectomorphic) identified by Sheldon and explain what ideas people tend to hold about individuals with each of these body types.

9. Summarize the explanations suggested for the apparent relationship between temperament and body type.

10. Describe individual differences in growth during middle childhood and the ways in which these differences could have a psychological impact.

11. Summarize what is known about the physical fitness of today's children and discuss whether the public schools should be held accountable for children's physical fitness.

REVIEWING THE CHAPTER

I. What is middle childhood?
   (pp. 451–453; study goal 1)

Middle childhood, which usually spans the years between 6 and 12, is marked by steady and sustained physical growth; mastery of more complex motor tasks; marked changes in thought, memory, and learning ability; growth in capacity for knowledge of the self and others; and formation of a child's first intimate friendships with people outside the family. Though the child generally has few responsibilities in this period, school begins and exposes him to new sets of people, social rules, and expectations to which his newfound abilities to consider others' points of view help him to adapt.

II. How do motor skills develop in middle childhood?
   (pp. 453–458; study goals 2 and 3)

Middle childhood presents sustained progress in development of fine motor skills as well as improvements in gross motor skills such as increased speed, power, coordination, balance, and agility. Ability to acquire new skills depends largely on opportunity for learning, encouragement, and practice. However, other factors, some genetic and physiological (e.g., body size, strength, and brain maturation) and some involving temperament and personality (e.g., energy level, venturesomeness, aggressiveness, persistence, and eagerness to participate in group functions) also affect the mastery of new motor skills. These new abilities enable children to participate in social and sports functions that provide an opportunity to interact with other children and adults with whom they may develop friendships and share interests.

During middle childhood, individual children vary widely in the execution of motor skills and mastery of complex motor tasks. Since minimal physical differences exist between the sexes at this point, age is more important than sex as a factor in the mastery of skills.

III. How does physical growth proceed in middle childhood?
   (pp. 458–473; study goals 4 to 7)

Physical growth in middle childhood proceeds slowly and evenly, permitting children to work on skills without the distraction of exhausting physical changes. In this period, children grow stronger and can go for longer periods without rest. Specific physical changes include increased skeletal and muscular growth, increased heart and lung capacity, and changes in body proportions as the child grows about

2.5 inches and gains about 5 pounds per year. In addition, loss of deciduous teeth continues throughout middle childhood and is associated with lengthening of the jaw and changes in facial proportions.

Individual children vary widely in physical growth and activity level, differences which exist in infancy and early childhood, but are accentuated during this period. At their extremes, variations in activity level may be classified as *attention deficit disorder* (ADD). This disorder, formerly labeled *hyperactive syndrome* or *minimal brain dysfunction,* encompasses both hyperactive and hypoactive behavior patterns. Hyperactivity, characterized by an inability to inhibit action, constant distraction by sounds and objects, a tendency to forget instructions, and difficulty with sequentially ordered behaviors, is more common in boys and tends to evoke anger and scolding from caretakers. The hypoactive child, who is more often female than male, exhibits less than normal activity levels and is often quite compliant, but is also unable to attend to specific tasks.

Various factors have been identified as potential causes of ADD. These include biological causes, such as prenatal infection or perinatal trauma, heredity, food additives and food allergies, and social explanations that stress the effects of having one's behavior labeled deviant. However, a complex interaction between social and biological causes may be at work.

Treatments for ADD are equally varied, including stimulants, behavior modification, psychotherapy, physical education, removal of distractions, and imposition of dietary restrictions. However, as yet there is no evidence that many of these treatments are effective. Proponents of stimulant treatment argue that it improves attentiveness, school work, and social performance. However, critics argue that stimulants may result in diminished appetite, weight loss, and interference with growth if used continuously. Other critics argue that these potentially addictive drugs do not enhance children's ability to learn and may be used as a substitute for real school reform.

Individual differences in growth, due to inheritance, nutrition, and physical and emotional health are especially apparent in the middle childhood years. Variation in height is particularly striking and even more so among children from different countries. The variations among generations reveal a secular trend toward earlier maturation. Thus, the onset of menarche and achievement of adult height are occurring sooner than they did in previous generations. Possible causes for these secular trends in height and sexual maturation include better nutrition, less subjection to illness, and some dominance in genes controlling stature. Children in middle childhood grow steadily taller, but there are no dramatic increases in height such as those characteristic of infancy and adolescence.

The secular trend toward earlier sexual maturation may have contributed to the recent rise in teen and preteen pregnancy. Other potential causes include: (1) societal changes that have encouraged sexual experimentation among children; (2) early sexual feelings combined with heavy pressure to conform with peers, who are engaging in sex with increased frequency; (3) lack of closeness between parents and children, making children more susceptible to peer influence; (4) later marriage, leaving a long gap between sexual maturation and marriage during which it may be unreasonable to expect abstention; and (5) ignorance of the hazards and consequences of sexual activity. Teenage pregnancy is an undesirable trend because teenage mothers are at risk for health complications, are often emotionally immature and ill-equipped to nurture their babies, and are five times more likely to leave school and less likely to find employment than other girls their age. Moreover, their infants are likely to show deficits in physical health and socioemotional and cognitive development. However, with the right support from adults, teen mothers are often able to continue their education and forestall repeated pregnancies. The probability of negative outcomes for their infants may be lessened by the presence of other adults in the home. Because there are so many potential causes of this problem, there is disagreement concerning how to prevent it. Some even argue that our society prefers a reactive approach to problems—choosing cure over prevention.

IV. How is physical growth related to psychological development?
(pp. 474–477; study goals 8 to 10)

What is the psychological significance of appearance? The increasing importance of peer relations combined with the wide individual differences in height and growth characteristic of this age period cause many children to feel sensitive about their physical appearance. In research that has sustained much methodological criticism, Sheldon identified three body types (endomorphic, mesomorphic, and ectomorphic), which he claimed were related to personality. However, other studies suggest that teachers and parents *do* seem to rate endomorphic girls as being more cooperative than ectomorphic girls and boys and to see mesomorphic boys as leaders. There are various explanations for any relationship that may exist between body type and personality. Perhaps differences in temperament result, in part, from the fact that individuals with different body types engage in different activities, which affect others' reactions to them. The relationship might also result from strong social stereotypes about the ways in which people with particular body types are supposed to behave. Preference for the mesomorphic type over the endomorphic type is present even among children and could cause some children to become dissatisfied with their own bodies, thereby provoking the negative behavior attributed to these body types.

SIGNIFICANT CONCEPTS, PEOPLE, AND TOPICS

You should become familiar with and be able to explain the following concepts, people, and topics. Most of the terms are highlighted in the margins of the text and some are also defined in the glossary at the end of the text.

secular trend   *fine motor skills*
gross motor skills   *motor fitness*
deciduous teeth   *hyperactivity*

hypoactivity
minimal brain dysfunction (MBD)
menarche
endomorphic
ectomorphic

hyperactive syndrome
attention deficit disorder (ADD)
William H. Sheldon
mesomorphic

SELF-CHECK

Choose the response that best answers the question or completes the statement.

_____ 1. Which of the following is *not* true of middle childhood?
  a. It is a time when the child grows in capacity for knowledge of the self and of the world.
  b. It is a time when children begin forming strong emotional ties with persons outside the family.
  c. It spans the years between 6 and 12.
  d. It is a time when most children experience a more pronounced growth spurt than in adolescence or infancy.

_____ 2. Which of the following body types seems to be consistently preferred by both children and adults?
  a. mesomorphic
  b. intramorphic
  c. endomorphic
  d. ectomorphic

_____ 3. Which of the following is usually the most important factor in the ability to acquire new motor skills during middle childhood?
  a. temperament and personality
  b. opportunity and practice
  c. body size
  d. strength

_____ 4. Attention deficit disorder (ADD) is a name given to
  a. the hyperactive, but not the hypoactive behavior pattern.
  b. the hypoactive, but not the hyperactive behavior pattern.
  c. both the hyperactive and hypoactive behavior patterns.
  d. none of the above

_____ 5. Which of the following has not been cited as a disadvantage of stimulant treatment for children with ADD?
  a. Stimulants may interfere with the immune system at a time when children are exposed to many illnesses.
  b. Stimulants are potentially addictive.
  c. Stimulants may cause diminished appetite or weight loss.
  d. Stimulants may be used as a substitute for school reform.

_____ 6. Secular trends indicate that
  a. the achievement of adult height is occurring later than in previous generations, but the onset of menarche occurs at a younger age than in the past.
  b. the onset of menarche occurs later than in previous generations, but the achievement of adult height occurs at a younger age than in the past.
  c. the onset of menarche and achievement of adult height are occurring sooner than they did in previous generations.
  d. the onset of menarche and the achievement of adult height are occurring later than they did in previous generations.

_____ 7. Which of the following is not true of teen and preteen pregnancy?
    a. Infants born to teen mothers often show deficits in physical health and socioemotional and cognitive development.
    b. Even with support from adults, teen mothers appear unable to forestall repeat pregnancies.
    c. Teen mothers are much more likely to leave school than other girls their age and are less likely to find employment.
    d. Teen mothers are at risk for health complications and are often ill-equipped to nurture their babies.

_____ 8. It has been difficult to prevent teen pregnancy because
    a. research shows that the most obvious solution, sexual education, promotes sexual behavior.
    b. there is disagreement concerning the cause of the problem and, consequently, disagreement about the best way to prevent it.
    c. there is little public awareness of the problem.
    d. the target population, teenage girls and boys, is difficult to reach.

_____ 9. Menarche is
    a. the event used to mark the onset of sexual maturity in females.
    b. sometimes followed by a short period of sterility.
    c. none of the above.
    d. both a and b.

_____ 10. Which of the following is *not* among the reasons cited for poor physical fitness among today's children?
    a. In times of austerity, physical fitness programs are often the first that schools elect to cut.
    b. There is little agreement about how to solve this problem and proposed solutions are difficult to implement.
    c. Today, children tend to prefer television viewing as a pastime.
    d. Schools are not held accountable for children's physical fitness.

Answers to Self-Check Questions

1. d	**6.** c
2. a	**7.** b
3. b	**8.** b
4. c	**9.** d
5. a	**10.** b

CHAPTER 11

COGNITIVE DEVELOPMENT DURING MIDDLE CHILDHOOD

STUDY GOALS

After reading and studying Chapter 11, you should be able to:

1. Describe the characteristics of the concrete operations period, defining *reversibility*, *decentering*, and *reciprocity*.

2. Explain why it is difficult for Piaget to account for horizontal decalage and summarize the explanations others have offered for this anomaly.

3. Summarize the beliefs and approach of neo-Piagetian researchers.

4. Describe the behavior of a child in the concrete operations period on class inclusion and seriation tasks.

5. List the potential explanations for variations between cultures in rates of cognitive development.

6. Describe Piaget's influence on education.

7. Contrast the Piagetian and information processing accounts of cognitive development, including a description of the components of thought.

8. Characterize the changes in attention, memory, and metamemory that occur in middle childhood.

9. List advances in language skills that occur during middle childhood and describe how some of these may be related to advances in cognitive skills.

10. Summarize the arguments for and against bilingual education.

11. Summarize the characteristics of schools and children that cause most cultures to begin formal schooling between the ages of 5 and 7.

12. Describe the factors, including learning disabilities, that affect acquisition of basic skills.

13. Contrast process and outcome evaluation.

14. Discuss the arguments made by proponents and opponents of mainstreaming as it has occurred under P.L. 94–142.

REVIEWING THE CHAPTER

I.   How does cognition change during the school-age years?
(pp. 481–500; study goals 1–8)

During middle childhood, between ages 7 and 12, children experience several cognitive changes that allow them to profit from formal schooling. In this period, children enter the *concrete operations* stage of cognitive development, characterized by more flexible thought than the preoperations period and the abilities to think logically, to organize ideas in a systematic fashion, and to avoid domination by immediate visual impressions. The child is now capable of performing *reversible mental operations* on concrete objects or signs of these objects, but not on hypothetical ideas, an ability which is reserved for adolescence. While the preoperational child considers only a single feature of an object at a time, the child in concrete operations can *decenter* to focus on multiple features of an object at the same time. He also exhibits understanding of *reciprocity,* the idea that a change in one feature of an object may be balanced by an equal and opposite change in another feature.

Grasp of these ideas and skills is demonstrated in the gradual acquisition of (in order of appearance) *conservation* of number, length, liquid quantity, mass, area, weight, and volume of objects and substances. The fact that different types of conservation, all based on the same principle, are acquired sequentially was referred to by Piaget as *horizontal décalage.* He did not think this anomaly was very important, but neo-Piagetians have explained it as a product of differences in experience with various materials or failure to generalize from one material to the next. In contrast to Piaget, neo-Piagetian researchers tend to focus on specific behaviors rather than global patterns and to claim that cognitive growth does not occur in stages at all.

With conservation of number comes a true understanding of one-to-one correspondence and class inclusion, which may not be present in every preschooler who can recite the counting numbers by rote. *Class inclusion,* or classification, is the ability to understand that there is a hierarchical relationship between subordinate and superordinate classes.

In addition to conservation, the cognitive operation of *seriation* emerges during this period, permitting the child to demonstrate systematic, planful thinking. *Transitive reasoning,* the ability to recognize a relationship between two objects by knowing their relationship to a third, is implicit in the ability to seriate.

Though Piaget attributes the emergence of transitive thinking to changes in cognitive structures, others argue that it is due to improved memory. Similarly, some researchers argue that preoperational children can solve class inclusion problems when they are presented in a way that avoids linguistic ambiguities.

On the basis of his observations of middle-class Western children, Piaget believed that children follow a universal and invariant sequence in cognitive development. Specifically, he argued that they progress sequentially through the sensorimotor, preoperational, and concrete operations stages, never skipping a stage since each stage lays the groundwork for the next. Cross-cultural studies confirm that children all over the world appear to follow this sequence. However, the rate at which children progress through the various stages differs among different cultures and within cultures, because of differences in environment and skills valued by other cultural groups. Studies by Gelman and others indicate that training may also accelerate children's acquisition of classification, transitive reasoning, and conservation. Piaget himself felt that cognitive progress was contingent on physiological maturation and interaction with the environment. Consequently, he argued that conceptual training only prevented the child from discovering the concept and hence from understanding it.

The notion of learning through discovery is basic to the *open classroom*, which surpasses the traditional classroom in promoting creativity and social interaction. However, researchers find that the traditional classroom appears to be superior for many academic tasks. There are, nonetheless, individual differences between teachers and students in the type of classroom in which they function best.

The *information processing* account of the development of thought offers an alternative to the Piagetian theory. This approach assumes that in order to understand their environment and learn to solve problems, children must encode what they see or hear, store this information, and retrieve it later to apply it to new experiences. Incremental improvements in these abilities are held responsible for changes in cognitive ability, which information processing theorists see as being *quantitative* rather than *qualitative*. Though there has been an explosion of studies on children's ability to attend to, store, and retrieve information, there is still no unified information processing theory of cognitive development.

Nonetheless, progress in attention and memory have been amply described. With age, *selective attention,* control over attentional processes, and length of concentration improve, permitting longer lessons in the later elementary grades. Problem solving is assisted by increases in the number and size of bits of information the child can remember. Finally, newfound classification skills enable the school-age child to use *organization* in addition to *rehearsal,* increasing the capacity for long-term memory. The school age child is also more aware of the need for such mnemonic devices, showing an intuitive understanding of memory, called *metamemory.*

II. How does linguistic ability develop during the school-age years? (pp. 500–507; study goal 9)

Metalinguistic awareness emerges at about age 5 and is enhanced throughout middle childhood as the child increases his communicative competence, ability to judge the clarity of messages, and ease in understanding syntactically complex sentences. School-age children are also less likely to confuse words than their preschool counterparts and they are able to appreciate metaphors; they see that words may have both literal and figurative meanings. Cognitive developments not only affect linguistic development, they enhance the appreciation of language devices, such as humorous riddles that depend on classification skills and reversible operations.

For some children, language becomes a barrier during the school-age years. Bilingual education, one approach to solving this problem, is criticized for drawing resources away from progress in English, which tends to be the criterion for success in our educational system. Supporters argue that the programs foster pride in cultural background and that their absence would cause non-English speakers to fall behind in basic skills. Similar obstacles are faced by black children from disadvantaged backgrounds; they may speak a dialect called *Black English,* which has grammar and pronunciation rules different from those of standard English.

III. The child in school: How do schools affect children?
     (pp. 507–524; study goals 10–14)

Much of middle childhood is spent in formal schooling, which requires the child to learn concepts set apart from their referents, to follow specific verbal instructions, and to adapt to a social dynamic in which she is limited in what she can say. In most societies, children begin formal schooling between 5 and 7, when they experience a set of cognitive changes that prepares them to profit from schooling. Studies in cultures in which schooling is not mandatory indicate that school improves memory and classification skills and enhances language development and word usage.

Various factors may influence acquisition and motivation to acquire skills. These include emotional problems, family conditions, values, parental encouragement, and specific problems such as dyslexia, childhood aphasia, dyscalculia, and hyperactivity. Federal efforts such as Follow Through have encouraged parental involvement because of its demonstrated effect on achievement.

The 1.8 million learning disabled school children are more likely than others to be rejected by peers or perceived negatively by teachers. There is disagreement over the cause of learning disabilities. Some point to prenatal and perinatal medical problems and others to a genetic mechanism. Whatever the cause, children do not outgrow learning disabilities, but learn to compensate for them. The most successful treatments attempt to deal with the manifestations of these problems rather than with their causes.

In the past, learning disabled and other handicapped children were taught in special classrooms. However, a recent law (P.L. 94–142) requires school systems to *mainstream* the majority of these children so they can be taught along with nonhandicapped children. The intent of the law is to provide handicapped children with equal educational opportunity. However, since there is at times a discrepancy between the intent of the law and the way in which it is put into practice, it remains for *process* and *outcome evaluations* to determine whether all mainstreamed handicapped children actually learn more than handicapped children who are not mainstreamed. Critics argue that many regular classroom teachers are not trained to deal with handicapped children, but proponents suggest that the law may reduce the stigma associated with handicapping conditions.

SIGNIFICANT CONCEPTS, PEOPLE, AND TOPICS

You should become familiar with and be able to explain the following concepts, people, and topics. Most of the terms are highlighted in the margins of the text and some are also defined in the glossary at the end of the text.

concrete operations period	mental operations
reversibility	operational thinking
decentering	reciprocity
conservation	conservation of mass
horizontal décalage	conservation of number
one-to-one correspondence	class inclusion
seriation	transitive reasoning
neo-Piagetian researchers	training studies
Rochel Gelman	open classroom
information processing	selective attention
sensory memory	short-term memory
long-term memory	mnemonic device
rehearsal	organization
metamemory	metalinguistic awareness
communicative competence	syntax
metaphor	bilingual education
Black English	basic skills
competence motivation	learned helplessness
Follow Through	learning disability
dyslexia	childhood aphasia
dyscalculia	hyperactivity
mainstreaming	Education for All Handicapped
process evaluation	Children Act (P.L. 94–142)
outcome evaluation	reflective cognitive style
impulsive cognitive style	Jerome Kagan
Matching Familiar Figures Test	

SELF-CHECK

Choose the response that best answers the question or completes the statement.

_____ 1. In most cultures, children begin formal schooling between ages 5 and 7 because
    a. children between 5 and 7 have longer attention spans and more advanced cognitive abilities than younger children.
    b. learning is particularly rapid at this age.
    c. children of this age have entered a critical period for knowledge acquisition.
    d. b and c

_____ 2. A child in the concrete operations period
    a. tends to show thought dominated by immediate visual impressions.
    b. can perform reversible mental operations on concrete objects or signs of these objects.
    c. can perform reversible mental operations on hypothetical ideas.
    d. considers only one feature of an object at a time.

_____ 3. Susan, 5, is presented with a picture showing 2 roses and 5 daisies. She is then asked, "Are there more daisies or more flowers?" and she responds, "More daisies." Susan's response is characteristic of the
    a. sensorimotor period.
    b. preoperational period.
    c. concrete operations period.
    d. formal operations period.

_____ 4. _Horizontal décalage_ refers to
    a. the ability to consider more than one feature of an object at the same time.
    b. the fact that different types of conservation are achieved sequentially rather than all at once.
    c. the ability to perform reversible mental operations.
    d. an information processing theory.

_____ 5. Neo-Piagetian researchers tend to
    a. concentrate on broad patterns of thought rather than individual behaviors.
    b. argue against the existence of stages of cognitive development.
    c. a and b
    d. none of the above

_____ 6. Which of the following is among the explanations suggested for horizontal déclalage?
    a. presence of methodological flaws in cross-cultural studies
    b. language problems built into the conservation task
    c. memory limitations
    d. differences in experience with various types of materials

_____ 7. As part of a program to improve reading achievement, teachers are trained in an instructional technique designed to enhance students' reading comprehension. Later, researchers are dispatched to monitor classes given by trained and non-trained teachers. The researchers rate the extent to which each teacher actually employs the technique. The rating activity is part of

 a. a process evaluation.
 b. an outcome evaluation.
 c. an open classroom.
 d. compliance with requirements imposed by P.L. 94–142.

____ 8. Which of the following is associated with Piaget's impact on education?

 a. achievement testing
 b. P.L. 94–142
 c. the open classroom
 d. the whole word method of reading instruction

____ 9. Unlike the Piagetian approach to cognitive development, the information processing approach

 a. has produced a unifying theory.
 b. emphasizes qualitative rather than quantitative change.
 c. a and b
 d. none of the above

____ 10. Cross-cultural studies find that children in some cultures

 a. do not achieve concrete operations.
 b. pass through Piagetian stages in a different order than children in the United States.
 c. pass through Piagetian stages at a different rate than children in the United States.
 d. all of the above

Answers to Self-Check Questions

1. a	**6.** d
2. b	**7.** a
3. b	**8.** c
4. b	**9.** d
5. b	**10.** c

CHAPTER 12

SOCIAL AND EMOTIONAL DEVELOPMENT
DURING MIDDLE CHILDHOOD

STUDY GOALS

After reading and studying Chapter 12, you should be able to:

1. Define the term *social cognition* and discuss the advances in social cognition that occur during the middle childhood years.

2. Define the term *role-taking* and discuss the developmental sequence of levels that children undergo in acquiring role-taking ability.

3. Explain why researchers think that social experience is an important aspect of role-taking ability.

4. Define the term *empathy* and explain why the ability for role-taking enhances the child's capacity for empathy.

5. Discuss the psychoanalytic, social learning, and cognitive-developmental explanations of moral development, and identify the two theorists who are well known for regarding moral development as a function of cognitive growth.

6. Explain two methods Piaget used to gain insight into children's perceptions of morality and discuss the different moral perceptions he identified among pre-schoolers and among children in the middle childhood period.

7. Know the 6 stages of moral development proposed by Kohlberg and discuss the value as well as the criticisms of Kohlberg's work.

8. Understand the distinction between moral knowledge and moral behavior and discuss social learning theorists' view on how children learn to behave in ways that are considered moral.

9. Discuss the two aspects of the self-concept—the child's definition of the self and the child's opinion of his own worth (that is, his self-esteem) which become increasingly refined during the middle childhood years.

10. Identify the influences of parents, teachers, and peers on the self-esteem and explain why the child's interactions with her parents are considered to be important in how the child will come to think of her own worth.

11. Know what is meant by the terms *academic curriculum* and *hidden curriculum* and explain the central role teachers play in the child's life.

12. Discuss some of the ways teachers influence not only the child but the child's parents as well.

13. Define the term *society of children* and explain why it is used to describe peer relations during the middle childhood years.

14. Know the changes that occur in children's peer group formation and discuss researchers' findings about children's need to conform to group norms.

15. Know the technique researchers use to identify popular children, identify the characteristics of popular children, and discuss the two other factors (sex and ethnicity) which, along with popularity, determine children's choices of friends.

16. Identify some of the realities of contemporary family life—dual-worker families, single-parent families, and poverty—which may interfere with parenting and explain their possible effects on children.

17. Define the term *latchkey children* and discuss some of the problems they and their parents face, and the possible solution to the problems.

18. Discuss the role corporations play in enhancing family life and some of the difficulties that may be encountered in this regard.

19. Explain what researchers have found out about children's ability to cope with stress.

REVIEWING THE CHAPTER

I.   What progress is made in social development during the middle childhood years? (pp. 526–532; study goals 1–4)

During the middle childhood years the child progresses in her ability to understand people and think about social relations. Referred to as social cognition, this ability is evident in several new developmental skills, including the acquisition of role-taking skills. Role-taking (also known as perspective-taking), is a cognitive skill which refers to the child's ability to comprehend how other people think and feel in different situations. This skill is acquired gradually over the early and middle childhood periods. Whereas preschoolers generally assume that other people's thoughts and feelings are identical to theirs, by the end of the middle childhood period children realize that other people may think or feel differently and they can also think about their own thoughts and feelings and those of other people simultaneously.

97

This ability greatly enhances the child's interactions with other people. Knowing that other people have their own particular values and interests and that they may view the world differently than she does, the child can communicate better (effective communication requires an understanding of others' perspectives), and she also acquires the capacity for empathy, the ability to understand and vicariously feel what another person is feeling. Although role-taking skills facilitate the child's social interactions in these ways, researchers have also found that social interactions are necessary if progress in role-taking is to occur. Apparently, children need the opportunity to interact with their peers if they are to become acquainted with how other people think and feel in different situations. Children who do not have the opportunity for peer interactions lag behind in their ability to see the perspective of others.

II. How do children learn the difference between right and wrong?
     (pp. 532–540; study goals 5–8)

During the middle childhood years the child also progresses in moral development and he acquires the ability to accept standards of right and wrong as guides to behavior. Several theories are offered to explain moral development. Psychoanalytic theorists claim that guilt is a major component of morality and that moral development is fostered by identification with the same-sex parent and the formation of the conscience, which serves to regulate the child's behavior. Social learning theorists contend that the child adopts standards of right and wrong as guides to behavior on the basis of cultural experiences and observations of and interactions with people.

The most popular explanation for the process of moral development is the one offered by cognitive-developmental theorists such as Jean Piaget and Lawrence Kohlberg, who emphasize that the development of morality is a function of cognitive growth. Piaget gained insights about children's moral development by asking children questions about the rules of a game. On the basis of the children's answers, Piaget noted that during the preschool period children perceive rules as sacred and unalterable even though they don't necessarily follow the rules as they play. During the middle childhood period, children become very strict about playing by the rules, and they expect all rules to be enforced. By the end of the period, they become more flexible and realize that since rules are formulated to benefit all those involved, they can be changed and reformulated with the consent of the participants.

Piaget also asked children questions about moral stories and he noted the developmental changes that occur in moral judgment. He found, for example, that younger children base their judgment of an act on the consequences involved whereas older children consider the intentions behind the act.

Kohlberg utilized a similar research method, asking children about different moral dilemmas. He found that as children grow older and acquire more refined cognitive skills, their moral judgments change. On the basis of his research, Kohlberg theorized that there are 6 (later revised to 5) stages of moral development, each building upon the other and each associated with changes in cognition. According to Kohlberg, these stages occur in an invariant order and are evident in children of different cultures.

Kohlberg's work has drawn attention to the developmental changes in moral judgment. However, not all researchers agree with his contentions. Some argue that his work is methodologically flawed since he based his findings on abstract moral dilemmas which have no relevance to children's real-life experiences. Others contend that Kohlberg failed to acknowledge the fact that women may base their moral decisions on different types of reasoning than do men, and the fact that moral development is enhanced through discussions and interactions with other people.

There are also researchers who draw a distinction between moral judgment and moral behavior. They emphasize the discrepancy that exists between beliefs and actions, noting that both children and adults do not always behave in ways that they think best. For example, a child may know that cheating on an exam is wrong, but depending on the circumstances may decide to cheat anyway. According to social learning theorists such as Aronfreed, approval by the adults who are important in the child's life is one of the most powerful reinforcers of moral behavior. He argues that as children learn what types of behavior bring approval or disapproval, they begin to think about their behavior in terms of the expected consequences.

Martin Hoffman also emphasizes the parents' role. He believes that depending on the disciplinary techniques parents utilize, children learn to behave morally and are encouraged to think about the consequences of their behavior.

III. How do children begin to feel good about themselves?
(pp. 540–550, 556–571; study goals 9–12, 16–19)

Parents also influence the child's attitudes about herself and her notion of how worthy she is. Although parental influence is evident throughout the childhood and adolescent years, it is especially important during the middle childhood period because during this period children acquire a more clearly defined notion of who they are (the self-concept) and how they feel about themselves (the self-esteem).

Children's self-esteem develops gradually during the middle childhood period and it is considered to be a vital aspect of the whole network of attitudes and beliefs that make up the self-concept. Children who feel good about themselves are usually motivated to succeed and to interact with other people. Children who have a low self-esteem regard themselves as inferior and unworthy of anyone's attention, and they shy away from social interactions, fearing they will be rejected.

Since the child's self-esteem is influenced by the parents, psychologists are concerned about stresses on family life which may interfere with effective parenting and have a negative influence on the child. Stresses on family life emanate from several recent trends, including the fact that in many families both parents work. The fact that both parents work is not, in and of itself, harmful to the child and can even be associated with some positive influences. However, in many cases, parents who work do not have adequate childcare arrangements, and they have to resort to leaving their children alone for several hours before and after school. These children are referred to as latchkey children because they sometimes wear their housekeys on a string around their necks.

Psychologists and child advocates contend that latchkey children should not stay home alone and that after-school day care arrangements should be made available to alleviate the stress that the children and their parents experience. Researchers have found that children can cope with stressful situations in their lives. However, when they experience more than one stressful situation at a time, their chances of overcoming these decrease. One of the contemporary problems we face as a society is related to the fact that many children experience multiple stresses that are brought on by the increase in poverty and in single-parent families.

Although parents play a vital role in how the child comes to regard herself, the self-esteem is influenced by other children and adults as well because during the middle childhood years the child's social world expands drastically as she begins formal schooling.

In school, the child is exposed to new role models, and she learns that she has to behave in ways that are valued and approved not only by her parents but by her peers and teachers as well. She also learns that there are different norms of behavior that define her role and the teacher's role. Some of these norms emanate from the academic curriculum. Others emanate from the hidden curriculum, which refers to the rules and regulations that govern interpersonal relations within the classroom.

How a child feels about herself in general and her school experience in particular is often determined by the teacher. Researchers have found that just as warm and accepting parents positively influence children's self-esteem, so teachers who are friendly and positively reinforcing influence how children feel about themselves and how motivated they are to succeed in school. Although the influence of the teacher on the child is evident, you should be aware that teachers influence parents as well. This is especially evident in the matter of discipline. Often, parents regard teachers as having knowledge about children's development and education, and many of them look to educators for guidance in regulating children's behavior.

IV. How do friendships develop?
(pp. 550–556; study goals 13–15)

The fact that children are at school means that they have more time to spend with one another. Not only do children spend more time with peers than ever before, they also form a society of children—a social world that is unique to children and has its own rituals, traditions, and activities.

This social world of children is evident in the formation of groups. Researchers have ascertained a developmental structure in group formation. During the beginning of the middle childhood years, groups are rather informal with no rules or regulations to define a hierarchy and facilitate interactions among members. At an older age, groups become more formal and children belong to fan clubs, nature clubs, or any other type of group that signifies structure and order. By the end of the period, children are less comfortable with groups, and they prefer instead to interact in informal cliques of two or three friends.

Children usually choose friends of the same sex and ethnic background, and they choose to be with children who are sociable, fun, and who get along with others. Psychologists have devised a research technique called sociometry to ascertain which children tend to be excluded from groups and which children are popular. They found that children tend to exclude from their groups any child who may seem to them to be odd or different in appearance or skills or whom they consider to be too low or too high in intelligence. They prefer to be with children who are moderately intelligent, outgoing, and socially sensitive.

Having friends and being with friends is very important to children during the middle childhood period so there is a tendency among children this age to imitate one another and conform to the behaviors of other children. Although children become increasingly susceptible to peer pressure, they are still very close to their family and subject to the care and influence of their parents.

SIGNIFICANT CONCEPTS, PEOPLE, AND TOPICS

You should become familiar with and be able to explain the following concepts, people, and topics. Most of the terms are highlighted in the margins of the text and some are also defined in the glossary at the end of the text.

social cognition
egocentric role-taking
self-reflective role-taking
empathy
moral development
conventional level of moral development
moral behavior
external control of behavior
punitive disciplinary techniques
self-esteem
industry vs. inferiority
hidden curriculum
society of children
cliques
sociogram
conformity to peers
latchkey children
corporal punishment
Lawrence Kohlberg
Martin Hoffman

role-taking ability
subjective role-taking
mutual role-taking
conscience
preconventional level of moral development
postconventional level of moral development
internal control of behavior
inductive disciplinary techniques
self-concept
academic curriculum
self-fulfilling prophecy
peer groups
sociometry
sex-cleavage
mental overload
school-age day care
Jean Piaget
Justin Aronfreed

SELF-CHECK

Choose the response that best answers the question or completes the statement.

_____ 1. According to Selman, a child who can realize that other people feel or think differently because they are in a different situation, but is unable to think about another person's perspective is in the _____ stage.
   a. subjective
   b. self-reflective role-taking
   c. egocentric
   d. mutual role-taking

_____ 2. A child's role-taking ability is influenced by her
   a. age.
   b. social experience.
   c. familiarity with people or situations.
   d. all of the above

_____ 3. In a cross-cultural study of Hungarian children's role-taking ability, Hollos found that children who lived _____ were not as capable in taking another person's perspective.
   a. in a town
   b. on a farm
   c. in a village
   d. none of the above, where children live does not influence their perspective taking ability

_____ 4. Although research indicates that _____ year old children can identify a happy face for happy stories, it is not until they are _____ years old that they can make inferences about other people's feelings.
   a. 4; 8
   b. 6; 8
   c. 8; 10
   d. 4; 12

_____ 5. Identify the statement about the development of moral knowledge that is _false_.
   a. The development of morality is a function of cognitive growth.
   b. Children are born with a moral code.
   c. According to Freud, guilt is a major component of morality.
   d. Moral behavior is shaped by cultural experience.

_____ 6. As children become older they understand that rules
   a. can be changed and reformulated through reasoning.
   b. are to be strictly followed.
   c. are unalterable.
   d. none of the above

_____ 7. Kohlberg has proposed that there are six stages of moral development. Put the following stages of moral judgment into the correct order.
   1. Behavior is motivated by the desire to take care of one's own needs.
   2. Behavior is motivated by the need to please people and gain approval.

3. Behavior is motivated by the need to avoid being punished.
4. Behavior is motivated by moral principles and recognition of universal concepts.
5. Behavior is motivated by doing one's duty and showing respect for others.
6. Behavior is motivated by a sense of obligation to societal or common good that has been mutually accepted.
   a. 3, 2, 1, 6, 5, 4
   b. 3, 1, 2, 5, 6, 4
   c. 2, 3, 1, 5, 4, 6
   d. 1, 2, 3, 4, 5, 6

____ 8. Younger children base their judgments of an act on the _____ ; whereas older children base their judgment on the _____ of the person involved.
   a. consequences; intentions
   b. accepted rules; intentions
   c. consequences; accepted rules
   d. intentions; consequences

____ 9. At about age _____ , peer groups are more formal and focus around shared interests and planned events.
   a. 13 years
   b. 11 years
   c. 9 years
   d. 6 to 7 years

____ 10. Studies indicate that quite often teachers base their expectations and assessment of a child's performance on
   a. the child's name.
   b. the child's intellectual ability.
   c. the child's social class or ethnic group
   d. a & c
   e. a, b, & c

Answers to Self-Check Questions

1. a	**6.** a
2. d	**7.** b
3. b	**8.** a
4. d	**9.** c
5. b	**10.** d

ATYPICAL DEVELOPMENT IN MIDDLE CHILDHOOD

STUDY GOALS

After studying the section on Atypical Development in Middle Childhood, you should be able to:

1. Describe the factors that should be considered in defining mental retardation and explain why one should not rely *only* on an IQ criterion.

2. List the four levels of severity of retardation and describe, in general terms, the types of accomplishments that can be expected at each level.

3. Contrast organic and cultural-familial retardation on the bases of frequency of occurrence, time of diagnosis, and severity.

4. Contrast the developmental perspective on mental retardation with the difference perspective and specify which approach places greater emphasis on the distinction between organic and cultural-familial retardation.

5. Summarize the changes in the approach to the care and education of the mentally retarded.

REVIEWING THE SECTION

Mental retardation, which is characterized by significantly subaverage levels of general intellectual functioning, is more common and easier to identify than other kinds of developmental psychopathology. In many cases, mental retardation is diagnosed at or shortly after birth. However, more often the handicap is not diagnosed until a child enters school and his intellectual performance is compared with others'.

The chief tool for diagnosing mental retardation has been the intelligence test, which has many problems that are outlined in Chapter 14. In addition to the problems associated with these tests, there is a certain arbitrariness in the designation of the IQ below which individuals will be labeled mentally retarded. The

American Association of Mental Deficiency (AAMD), which sets this criterion, has raised and lowered it at various times since 1959. This arbitrariness alerts us to the error in rigidly adhering to such cutoff points that draw the defining line between mental retardation and normal intellectual functioning. Other considerations in defining mental retardation are an individual's deficits in adaptive behavior and his ability to meet the standards of independence and responsibility imposed on a person of his age and cultural group.

Even those identified as retarded vary widely in their mental functioning and can be differentiated on the basis of the severity of retardation—mild (IQ 55 to 69), moderate (IQ 40 to 54), severe (IQ 25 to 39), or profound (IQ below 25). In fact, most mentally retarded individuals are only mildly impaired and are still able to meet their own needs, hold jobs, and manage a household with minimal aid.

One may also differentiate among the retarded on the basis of etiology. From this perspective, two types of mental retardation are identified: retardation caused by a known *organic* disorder and retardation with an unknown organic disorder, often called *cultural-familial retardation*. Approximately 20 to 25% of retardation is associated with one of over 200 known organic causes, which result in impaired physiological development. These causes include genetic or chromosomal anomalies, diseases inherited genetically, and prenatal brain damage due to maternal rubella, lead poisoning, nutritional deficiencies, perinatal oxygen deprivation, or cerebral trauma. Generally, *organic* retardation is diagnosed shortly after birth or during infancy and tends to result in severe or profound impairment.

Approximately 75 to 80% of the mentally retarded fall into the cultural-familial category and may not show noticeably slow development before entering school. These children appear to be normal, except that they perform at a mentally retarded level, learn slowly, show little interest in their school surroundings, have poor communication skills, are immature in their behavior, and tend to fall further behind their peers with each year in school. Cultural-familial retarded children are usually classified as mildly retarded. Though it is generally agreed that cultural-familial retardation results from a combination of environmental (cultural) and hereditary (familial) factors, the relative contribution of each of these factors is still the subject of controversy.

There are also different theoretical approaches to mental retardation. The *developmental perspective* argues that those with organic problems are fundamentally different. However, this perspective contends that cultural-familial retarded children should not be viewed as different, because they develop in the same sequence of stages as normal children and differ only in the rate at which they progress and the ultimate level attained. This perspective also claims that cultural-familial retarded children react to the environment in the same way as normal children. Thus, the rigidity, overdependence, and low expectancy of success often associated with the retarded are attributed to these children's experiences (e.g., frequent failure) rather than to a defect inherent in retardation. In contrast, the *difference,* or *defect, perspective* argues that *all* retarded children suffer from either circumscribed (e.g., impaired memory, attention deficiencies) or pervasive, physiological impairments that make them fundamentally different from normal children.

Experts disagree on the best way to care for and educate retarded children. The severely or profoundly retarded are often institutionalized when their handicap is diagnosed or when their families can no longer handle their care. However, mildly or moderately retarded children usually remain with their families and receive educational training, through which 50 to 80% eventually become self-supporting. This emphasis on mainstreaming and normalization has replaced the practice of indiscriminately placing retarded children in separate and often ineffective residential centers.

SIGNIFICANT CONCEPTS AND TOPICS

You should become familiar with and be able to explain the following concepts and topics. Most of the terms are highlighted in the margins of the text and some are also defined in the glossary at the end of the text.

mental retardation	*mild retardation*
moderate retardation	*severe retardation*
profound retardation	*organic retardation*
cultural-familial retardation	*difference/defect perspective*
developmental perspective	*normalization*

SELF-CHECK

Choose the response that best answers the question or completes the statement.

_____ 1. The defect perspective maintains that
   a. retarded children pass through the same developmental sequence as other children.
   b. one should make a sharp distinction between the organically retarded and the cultural-familial retarded.
   c. all retarded children are fundamentally different from normal children.
   d. cultural-familial retarded children respond to the environment in the same way as other children.

_____ 2. Organically retarded children
   a. tend to be severely or profoundly retarded.
   b. are usually not diagnosed before entering school.
   c. are more likely to be able to work and live independently than other retarded children.
   d. all of the above

_____ 3. Most retarded individuals
   a. are organically retarded.
   b. live in residential centers for the mentally retarded.
   c. are identified in infancy.
   d. none of the above

_____ 4. Cultural-familial retardation
   a. characterizes only a small number of retarded individuals.
   b. is usually identified in infancy.
   c. is associated with a known physiological disorder.
   d. characterizes more mildly retarded individuals than organic retardation.

_____ 5. Martin, who has an IQ of 60, is able to make change and has a job where he is closely supervised. Martin is most likely to have been diagnosed as
   a. moderately retarded.
   b. mildly retarded.
   c. profoundly retarded.
   d. severely retarded.

_____ 6. *Normalization* refers to
   a. the argument, made by developmental theorists, that cultural-familial retarded children pass through the same sequence of stages as normal children.
   b. the argument, made by difference theorists, that cultural-familial retarded children pass through the same sequence of stages as normal children.
   c. current educational approaches that stress allowing retarded children to develop in as normal an environment as possible.
   d. none of the above

Answers to Self-Check Questions

1. c	**3.** d	**5.** b
2. a	**4.** d	**6.** c

CHAPTER 13

PHYSICAL DEVELOPMENT DURING ADOLESCENCE

STUDY GOALS

After reading and studying Chapter 13, you should be able to:

1. Define adolescence by indicating when it begins and when it ends.

2. Describe the cultural factors that have led to the invention of adolescence and those that are extending its length.

3. List the explanations that have been offered for emotional difficulties once thought to be characteristic of adolescence and discuss whether adolescent difficulties are due to biological or cultural factors.

4. Contrast the views on adolescence expressed by Hall, Mead, Lewin, and Bandura.

5. Explain what recent research has found about the stressful nature of adolescence and the emotional characteristics of adolescents.

6. Describe the chain of physiological events that results in production and secretion of sex hormones.

7. Describe how hormone production rises and falls between the prenatal period and the onset of puberty.

8. Explain how the hormonal changes during puberty differ for boys and girls.

9. List the ways in which nutritional needs change during puberty and name some of the obstacles adolescents face in meeting these new needs.

10. Describe anorexia nervosa, bulimia, and the characteristics and possible causes of these disorders.

11. Describe the changes associated with sexual maturity in males and females (i.e., identify the hormonal and internal events that precede menarche and ejaculation).

12. List secondary sexual characteristics that develop during puberty in males and females and describe the sex differences in hair growth and shoulder, hip, breast, and voice development.

13. Explain how blackheads, whiteheads, and acne develop, describe the role of androgens in this process, and differentiate between factors that cause acne and those that appear only to aggravate previously existing acne.

14. Summarize the evidence linking hormones and behavior.

15. Describe the findings of the California Growth Study regarding the short- and long-term consequences of early and late maturation in male and female adolescents.

16. Summarize the trends in adolescent depression and suicide and list the characteristics and dangers associated with adolescent depression.

17. Name a few of the precipitating events or warning signals associated with adolescent suicide and characterize the accuracy of these indicators.

REVIEWING THE CHAPTER

I. What is adolescence?
(pp. 583–587; study goals 1–4)

For the purpose of our discussion, we define adolescence as the period between 12 and 18. However, it is actually an ill-defined stage of life that begins with puberty and lasts until the individual makes the transition to adulthood. One reason that adolescence is difficult to define is that it is a cultural invention that has only been regarded as a separate period of life since the late 19th century. At that time, the forces of industrialization, compulsory schooling, and child labor legislation combined to highlight the need for education and to promote the dependence of youth on adult care. Recently, adolescence has become even longer because children mature earlier physically, they are exposed earlier to adult aspects of life, and they are required by societal needs to obtain more and more schooling.

Several theorists have attempted to explain the rebelliousness and emotional turmoil often taken to characterize adolescence. Some emphasize the difficulty of handling a mature body and social and psychological characteristics that are seen as immature. Others point to the lack of psychological support given to adolescents assuming adult roles and the lack of agreement in our society on the point at which an individual is regarded as an adult.

G. Stanley Hall regarded what he called the "storm and stress" of adolescence as the outcome of biological causes. However, Margaret Mead argued that cultural factors were responsible for adolescent difficulties, since adolescence seemed to be a trouble-free time in Samoa. Though Mead's conclusions have been challenged on methodological grounds, others have also presented cultural explanations for adolescent turmoil. Kurt Lewin likened adolescent behavior to that of members of minority groups dealing with feelings of marginality and Bandura argues that social expectations that adolescents will be rebellious and unpredictable may force adolescents into this role.

II. How does the body change during adolescence?
   (pp. 587–600; study goals 5–14)

The hormonal changes in adolescence culminate in sexual maturity, reproductive capability, and the emergence of secondary sexual characteristics. These changes begin when the pituitary gland secretes hormones into the bloodstream that subsequently stimulate other endocrine glands, such as the adrenals, ovaries, and testes to produce sex hormones. Though sex hormones are present in great quantities in both sexes during the prenatal period, their production is suppressed until approximately age 7, when levels begin to rise gradually. Between ages 10 and 12, levels of these hormones increase rapidly and stimulate puberty.

The growth spurt characteristic of adolescence begins with weight gain followed by rapid increases in height and redistribution of fat. For boys, this period of rapid growth usually begins near age 13, two years later than it begins in girls. Among the less obvious changes accompanying the growth spurt are the thickening of the lips; the growth of the hands, feet, and legs; and the disappearance of childhood facial features with diminishing head growth and widening of the forehead and mouth. In addition, there is a spurt of muscle growth and a decrease in the proportion of body tissue composed of fat, which remains lower for males even into adulthood. Other physical changes accompanying puberty are decreased heart rate, continued heart growth, and increased lung capacity. These changes enable adolescents to engage in activities requiring endurance and to perfect motor skills developed in middle childhood.

Since muscle development is accompanied by increases in strength, these are greater and remain greater for boys because of their higher muscle-to-fat ratios. Sexual differences in physical growth, which are pronounced in adolescence, also include differences in size, heart rate, lung capacity, and weight gain.

Growth is accompanied by metabolic changes that increase appetite and by an increased need for calories, protein, and specific minerals and vitamins. However, adolescents are often deficient in certain minerals, because they face such obstacles to proper nutrition as misinformation about food values, interest in group activities that often occur during mealtimes and, among girls, increased food needs at a time of heightened desire for slimness. Not coincidentally, anorexia nervosa and bulimia occur largely among adolescent girls. The anorexic, characterized by bizarre attitudes toward food, distorted body image, and self-induced starvation, often experiences loss of more than 25% of normal body fat, cessation of menstruation, weakness, and muscle deterioration. Five to 15% of anorexics starve to death and, without treatment, only half improve. Some success has been achieved with psychotherapy and behavior modification techniques. Among the suggested causes of anorexia are psychological need to avoid adulthood, rejection of the mother, presence of an overcontrolling mother, and faulty body image related to a misguided societal ideal of feminine beauty.

Sexual changes begin as estrogen and androgen production rise in males and females. These hormonal changes are responsible for the development of secondary sexual characteristics as well as changes in the reproductive organs. In females, cyclic estrogen production and other hormonal events precipitate enlargement of the uterus, thickening of .he vaginal lining, and menarche, which marks the beginning of reproductive potential. Actual reproductive capacity may lag behind menarche by six months to a year depending on when ovulation begins. In males, hormonal changes promote the growth and thickening of the penis, enlargement of the scrotal sac, and the beginning of ejaculation. If a sufficient concentration of live, motile sperm are present in the seminal fluid, ejaculation signals the beginning of male reproductive capability.

Hormones also trigger changes in physique—boys develop wide shoulders and relatively narrow hips and girls develop wider, more rounded hips and narrow shoulders. Girls also begin breast development during this period. Even in boys, breasts become larger and the areola grows in diameter. In both sexes, head and body hair become darker and coarser. New and gradually denser hair growth appears in the pubic and axillary areas and, among boys, in the facial and chest areas. As the larynx enlarges and vocal cords lengthen, both sexes also experience a lowering of the voice, but this is more dramatic in boys, for whom it is called the breaking of the voice.

Hormones also affect the skin, the sex drive, and possibly emotions and behavior. For instance, acne is caused by sebum production from glands in the skin stimulated by increased androgen levels. This skin disorder is a common condition among adolescents, which may be exacerbated, but not caused, by poor eating habits or hygiene. Since children of acne sufferers are likely to be affected, there may be a genetic component involved as well. Some argue that *cyclic* hormonal changes are responsible for the temporary mood changes, depression, and fatigue associated with premenstrual syndrome. However, vitamin deficiencies may be partly to blame for these problems. Another example of the impact of hormonal changes is the link between male sex drive and high levels of androgen secretion, which may also affect female sex drive. Animal studies indicate that the relationship between hormones and behavior may work in both directions; behavior may influence hormone levels as well as vice versa.

III. What are the psychological effects of these changes?
   (pp. 600–607; study goals 15–17)

The timing of maturation can have psychological significance for some adolescents. In the United States, where physical characteristics are highly valued by young boys, early or late maturation has a long-lasting impact on behavior. Over the short term, early maturing boys tend to have positive self-esteem, to be treated by adults as more mature, and to show little need to strive for status. Early maturing girls, on the other hand, tend to feel embarrassed and isolated until other girls catch up, when the early maturers begin to enjoy increased popularity with both sexes. Over the long term, no differences are found between adult women who matured early and those who matured late. However, in males, the effects of early maturation are long-lasting. Even though no physical differences persisted into adulthood, early maturing males in the California Growth Study tended to be more cooperative, enterprising, and conforming adults than their late-maturing counterparts. Late-maturing boys and girls tend to have lower self-esteem and they tend to be more active attention-seekers than early maturers. As adults, late-maturing males are more rebellious, touchy, self-assertive, and solicitous of others' aid and encouragement.

Adolescents face many challenges, including acquisition of self-identity and independence, formation of close social and sexual relationships outside the family, and formation of important career decisions. These tasks may produce stress that manifests itself in early adolescence as poor self-concept or quarelling with parents. Depression, characterized by fatigue, inactivity, difficulty in concentrating, and deep sadness, shows a marked rise in incidence associated more closely with puberty than with chronological age. Recently, there has also been an increase in adolescent suicide, which is now the third leading cause of death in this age group, after accidents and homicide. Although there is little agreement among researchers on the causes of adolescent suicide, there are several warning signs that can serve as imperfect guides to those seeking to offer help.

SIGNIFICANT CONCEPTS, PEOPLE, AND TOPICS

You should become familiar with and be able to explain the following concepts, people, and topics. Most of the terms are highlighted in the margins of the text and some are also defined in the glossary at the end of the text.

puberty	*sexual differentiation*
adolescence	*puberty rites*
G. Stanley Hall	*Margaret Mead*
Kurt Lewin	*Albert Bandura*
hormones	*androgens*
testosterone	*estrogen*
secondary sexual characteristics	*pituitary gland*
master gland	*hypothalamus*
endocrine glands	*adrenal glands*
ovaries	*testes*
growth spurt	*iron deficiency anemia*
anorexia nervosa	*bulimia*
menarche	*ejaculation*
areola	*axillary*
breaking of the voice	*acne*
sebum	*premenstrual syndrome*
sex drive	*double standard*
California Growth Study	*depression*

SELF-CHECK

Choose the response that best answers the question or completes the statement.

_____ 1. Which of the following events defines the beginning of adolescence?
   a. age 12
   b. puberty
   c. age 13
   d. androgen or estrogen production

_____ 2. In recent years, adolescence has become
   a. longer, because of the job requirements of an industrialized society.
   b. longer, because children mature later physically.
   c. shorter, because children mature earlier physically.
   d. shorter, because of the job requirements of an industrialized society.

_____ 3. There have been many attempts to explain the emotional turmoil taken to be characteristic of adolescence. Which of the following theorists regarded the adolescent's behavior as being primarily the outcome of _biological_ causes?
   a. Margaret Mead
   b. Kurt Lewin
   c. G. Stanley Hall
   d. Albert Bandura

_____ 4. The following list includes three events that form part of the physiological sequence leading to the production of sex hormones. Select the choice that places these physiological events in chronological order. (1) The hypothalamus stimulates the pituitary gland to produce hormones. (2) The ovaries and testes produce androgen and estrogen. (3) The master gland releases hormones into the bloodstream.
   a. 1, 2, 3
   b. 1, 3, 2
   c. 3, 2, 1
   d. 3, 1, 2

_____ 5. Which of the following is _not_ among the consequences of anorexia nervosa?
   a. loss of large portions of _normal_ body fat
   b. cessation of menstruation
   c. severe and chronic dehydration
   d. weakness and muscle deterioration

_____ 6. All of the following are characteristic elements of the adolescent growth spurt _except_
   a. enlargement of hands, feet, and legs.
   b. weight loss.
   c. lowering of the forehead.
   d. diminishment of head growth relative to other skeletal growth.

_____ 7. Muscular development in adolescence
   a. is more rapid in boys than girls, resulting in lower fat-to-muscle ratios and greater strength in boys.

113

b. is *equally* rapid for boys and girls, resulting in approximately equal fat-to-muscle ratios for the two sexes.

c. is slower for girls, but girls eventually attain fat-to-muscle ratios equivalent to boys'.

d. is more rapid in girls, but eventually slows, causing boys' fat-to-muscle ratios to surpass girls'.

____ 8. In boys, reproductive potential begins with _____ , but actual reproductive capability also requires _____

a. ejaculation, androgen production.

b. puberty, androgen production.

c. androgen production, a sufficient concentration of live, motile sperm.

d. ejaculation, a sufficient concentration of live, motile sperm.

____ 9. Late-maturing boys and girls tend to

a. avoid attention from peers and adults.

b. attract teasing from early-maturing peers.

c. show little status-consciousness.

d. exhibit at least temporarily low self-esteem.

____ 10. Adolescent suicide

a. is a new phenomenon unheard of before 1950.

b. is attempted more often by girls, but accomplished more often by boys.

c. is the leading cause of death in this age group.

d. can be accurately predicted by those who know the warning signs.

Answers to Self-Check Questions

1.	b	**6.**	b
2.	a	**7.**	a
3.	c	**8.**	d
4.	b	**9.**	d
5.	c	**10.**	b

CHAPTER 14

COGNITIVE DEVELOPMENT DURING ADOLESCENCE

STUDY GOALS

After reading and studying Chapter 14, you should be able to:

1. List at least five ways in which the adolescent's thought (formal operations) differs from that of the child (concrete operations).

2. Describe Inhelder's and Piaget's pendulum problem and the way in which a child in the formal operations period would attempt to solve it.

3. Name the factors which appear to encourage or inhibit the display of formal operations.

4. Summarize the characteristics of adolescent egocentrism and explain how this is different from preschool egocentrism.

5. List some of the criticisms directed at the practice of tracking.

6. Describe the arguments for and against the use of achievement and aptitude tests to assign students to tracks.

7. Contrast the Piagetian and psychometric approaches.

8. Discuss the history of the debate over whether there is one basic intelligence or many separate abilities and describe the views of Spearman and Thurstone.

9. Describe the extent of agreement on a definition of intelligence and the various attempts to subdivide the concept.

10. List the criteria which an intelligence test must meet in field testing and describe the factors one must consider in selecting a standardization sample.

11. Recount the history of IQ testing, including the purpose of the first test, the work of Binet and Simon, and the extension of their work by Terman and Wechsler.

12. Define the concept of mental age and explain how the intelligence quotient improved upon this measure.

13. List some factors other than aptitude that may affect intellectual performance.

14. List at least three explanations that have been offered for the relationship between IQ and socioeconomic status.

15. Summarize the evidence offered to support or refute the notions that IQ tests are biased toward white, middle-class culture and that the relation between IQ and socioeconomic status is traceable to genetic differences between the middle and lower classes.

16. Discuss the role of heredity and environmental factors in determining intellectual performance.

17. List some characteristics of those schools that have succeeded in improving academic performance, behavior, and attendance.

18. Discuss factors that have prevented implementation of compensatory education programs at the high school level and describe the need for such programs; include a discussion of illiteracy, truancy, and nonenrollment.

REVIEWING THE CHAPTER

I. How does thought change during adolescence?
(pp. 610–613; study goals 1–3)

During adolescence, many individuals enter the fourth and last of Piaget's stages of cognitive development, the period of *formal operations*. Not all adolescents attain this stage, but those who do show thought that differs from the child's *concrete operations* in at least five ways. First, the adolescent can think abstractly and can logically manipulate statements as well as things. Second, he can entertain hypotheses, because he has mastered *interpropositional logic*—the knowledge that the same logical rules can be applied to hypothetical problems that he previously used with concrete problems. Third, the formal operations individual is capable of thinking ahead and planning a strategy rather than relying on trial and error. Fourth, the formal operations thinker is capable of reflective thinking, which Piaget called performing *operations on operations* and which information processing theorists label *metacognition*. This permits the adolescent to improve his thought processes and to gauge the strength of his ideas. Finally, the adolescent thinks about a wider variety of topics than the child and considers them in greater depth. The adolescent's ability to adopt a scientific method of problem solving can be shown by performance on the chemistry or pendulum problems, classic experiments conceived by Inhelder and Piaget to illustrate the gradual development of logic.

Even in cultures with compulsory schooling, many individuals do not attain formal operations. In nontechnological societies, nonattainment of formal operations is the rule rather than the exception. However, anthropological evidence indicates that this may be attributable to the unfamiliar Piagetian tasks used to measure cognitive development. Individuals in nontechnological societies *do* show the characteristics of formal operations thought in tasks relevant to their way of life. Motivational and environmental factors may also affect displays of formal operations, since adolescents are most likely to demonstrate formal operations in areas in which they are knowledgeable.

II. What is adolescent egocentrism?
(pp. 614–615; study goal 4)

In early adolescence, individuals may also display *adolescent egocentrism.* Unlike the preschooler, the adolescent acknowledges that others have their own thoughts, which may differ from his own, but has a tendency to believe that he alone experiences intense feelings and often feels misunderstood. The egocentric adolescent creates an *imaginary audience* for himself, which explains the self-consciousness of early adolescence. Along with this goes a *personal fable,* a belief that because everyone is interested in oneself, one must be special. This can promote personal strength, but may also lead to a sense of indestructability and excessive risk taking. At about age 15 or 16, when task orientation begins to become important to the adolescent and when he has had an opportunity to spend time discussing beliefs with others, the characteristics of adolescent egocentrism disappear.

III. How does schooling affect personal and cognitive development?
(pp. 618–639; study goals 5–18)

In high school, the adolescent studies more varied subjects in greater depth. Since many adolescents have entered the formal operations period and others may do so, instruction that draws on abilities to consider abstract notions will be more stimulating than instruction that ignores these abilities.

In an effort to deal with differences in intellectual performance, *achievement* and *aptitude* tests are used to compare students against group *norms* and assign them to a track. These assignments often determine the type of courses they take and can affect their direction in life, their feelings about themselves, and the way others regard them. *Tracking* is criticized for causing inequalities in instruction. For instance, high track classes receive more instruction, are assigned more homework, focus on higher level skills, and are less likely to encourage passivity than middle or low track classes.

Controversy also surrounds the use of tests to evaluate students. Proponents contend that scores accurately reflecting intellectual ability can be useful to those who strive to help children reach their learning potential. Critics argue that the tests are used to exclude children from opportunities rather than to provide such opportunities and that test scores are used to make decisions too important to rest on such partial information. This focus on individual differences is part of the *psychometric approach* rather than the *Piagetian approach.* The latter concentrates on qualitative differences over time and employs interview techniques to investigate the reasoning behind children's responses.

Psychologists don't agree on a definition for intelligence, but do agree that there are at least two aspects of intelligence: *intellectual potential* (Hebb's *intelligence*

117

A) and *intellectual performance* (Hebb's *ingelligence B)*. Similarly, Cattell and Horn differentiated between *fluid intelligence,* or basic mental abilities relatively uninfluenced by prior learning, and *crystallized intelligence,* or knowledge influenced by experience, cultural background, and education. Historically, psychologists have debated whether there is one, basic intelligence similar to Spearman's *g* that affects performance on many tasks or many, separate abilities required for specific tasks, similar to Spearman's *s* factors. Thurstone suggested that the intellect consisted of *seven primary mental abilities,* but found that scores on tests of these separate abilities tended to be interrelated, which strengthened the argument for one, general factor of intelligence.

Depending on the operative definition of intelligence, intelligence tests may contain different types of items. However, the tests must be both *valid* and *reliable.* After these qualities have been demonstrated through field testing, the test is *standardized.* The larger and more representative the standardization sample, the more widely applicable the test will be. Although the IQ test may not be a good measure of intelligence, it is relied upon as a measure of intellectual performance, because IQ scores have proven to be good predictors of scholastic success.

In fact, Alfred Binet and Theophile Simon developed the first IQ test in order to identify mentally retarded students for special instruction. Binet and Simon assessed *mental age* (MA) by presenting items in ascending order of difficulty. However, MA alone did not facilitate comparison of children of different ages. This was made possible by Stern's development of the IQ score (MA/CA × 100 = IQ), a measure that remains relatively constant over time. Today, more advanced statistical methods are used to compute IQs.

Binet's and Simon's test was revised and restandardized for use with English speaking children by Lewis Terman at Stanford University. However, the *Stanford-Binet* relies as heavily on culturally laden verbal skills as its predecessor. Other, culture-fair tests have been developed to avoid this problem. These include the *Wechsler Adult Intelligence Scale* (WAIS), the *Wechsler Intelligence Scale for Children* (WISC), and the *Wechsler Preschool and Primary Scale of Intelligence* (WPPI), which yield scores for both *verbal IQ* and *performance IQ.* Though verbal IQ is a better predictor of scholastic success, performance IQ is considered a more valid measure of aptitude.

What *isn't* measured by IQ scores? IQ scores predict school success and later occupational success with adequate, but not perfect, accuracy. However, they are less useful in predicting everyday adult functioning and do not measure adaptation to life circumstances—Piaget's definition of intelligence. The IQ test measures intellectual performance rather than intellectual ability and this performance is affected by many factors, including aptitude, achievement motivation, parental encouragement, emotional status, reading ability, test-taking skills, ease in the test-taking situation, and perhaps even *impulsive* or *reflective cognitive style.*

Various explanations have been offered for the apparent relationship between IQ and socioeconomic level (income). The first is that schools encourage the achievements valued by white, middle-class families and that the tests themselves are biased toward knowledge that is more available to white, middle-class children. Another explanation for the relationship between IQ and socioeconomic status is that persons from different income backgrounds may have different levels of motivation to succeed on tests. Since children from various ethnic backgrounds excel in different mental abilities, the idea, suggested by Jensen, that the relationship between IQ and socioeconomic status is due to genetic differences in ethnic groups has been rejected by most investigators. In addition, low-income ethnic groups show parallel, but lower, scores when compared to middle-class ethnic group members, which demonstrates the significance of economic deprivation.

Studies of identical and fraternal twins have shown that both heredity and environment affect intellectual performance. The importance of environmental factors is demonstrated by the fact that even children from the same family differ in IQ depending on such factors as birth order, family size, and spacing between children. One study indicates that an individual's IQ can be increased by as much as 10 to 20 points by living in a middle-class home and there is evidence that early compensatory education may have been effective in raising IQ.

There have been few efforts to help high school students with low IQs, because compensatory education has traditionally concentrated on younger children and the most capable of the economically disadvantaged and because of the widely held belief that adolescence is too late to overcome educational handicaps. However, evidence from Reuven Feuerstein's work indicates that a program of mediated experiences guiding children toward acquisition of basic cognitive skills can successfully increase IQ even among some adolescents. Though Feuerstein's program emphasizes expensive individual instruction, it holds the promise of avoiding later costs to society. The need for such compensatory education is underscored by the fact that 17–21 million Americans are functionally illiterate and 46 million cannot read proficiently. Because of rising illiteracy and lawsuits for educational malfeasance, some states have tightened graduation requirements and ended social promotions. However, these isolated steps may do more to prevent high school graduation than to prevent illiteracy.

Although schooling is both free and mandatory in the United States, over 1 million children between 7 and 15 years of age do not attend. Nonenrollees are likely to be poor, non-white, and non-English speaking. The number of truants has also increased and these students tend to have underdeveloped academic skills, negative self-concepts, negative attitudes toward school subjects, stressful family situations, economic anxiety, and few satisfying experiences with teachers or fellow students. Though many school officials have taken a punitive approach to truancy, this may yield no positive effect and may promote further rebellion and dropping out.

Studies by Michael Rutter and others indicate that schools that do succeed in increasing attendance and achievement tend to be schools that encourage parent involvement, collect homework assignments, maintain an academic emphasis, offer students opportunities for responsibility, promote good conditions for students, and emphasize continuity of the school population.

SIGNIFICANT CONCEPTS, PEOPLE, AND TOPICS

You should become familiar with and be able to explain the following concepts, people, and topics. Most of the terms are highlighted in the margins of the text and some are also defined in the glossary at the end of the text.

Jean Piaget

interpropositional logic

metacognition

metamemory

Inhelder's and Piaget's chemistry problem

achievement testing

tracking

psychometric approach

intelligence quotient (IQ)

intellectual behavior

intelligence B

fluid intelligence

verbal intelligence

practical intelligence

g factor

Louis Leon Thurstone

validity

field testing

Alfred Binet

William Stern

Stanford-Binet Test

Wechsler Adult Intelligence Scale (WAIS)

Wechsler Preschool and Primary Scale of Intelligence (WPPI)

cognitive style

reflective style

Arthur R. Jensen

mediated learning experiences

Michael Rutter

imaginary audience

formal operations period

performing operations on operations

metalinguistics

scientific method of problem solving

Inhelder's and Piaget's pendulum problem

aptitude testing

norms

Piagetian approach

intellectual potential

intelligence A

D. O. Hebb

crystallized intelligence

problem-solving ability

Charles E. Spearman

s factor

primary mental abilities

reliability

standardization

Theophile Simon

Lewis Terman

David Wechsler

Wechsler Intelligence Scale for Children (WISC)

verbal IQ

performance IQ

impulsive style

culture-fair tests

Reuven Feuerstein

truancy

adolescent egocentrism

personal fable

SELF-CHECK

Choose the response that best completes the statement or answers the question.

_____ 1. Which of the following terms comes closest to the meaning of *metacognition?*
   a. interpropositional logic
   b. formal operations
   c. operations on operations
   d. cognitive style

_____ 2. Research indicates that all of the following factors are associated with the display of formal operations *except*
   a. genetic preparedness.
   b. familiarity with the task.
   c. exposure to schooling.
   d. the society's level of technological development.

_____ 3. The personal fable
   a. usually appears in late adolescence.
   b. can lead to excessive risk-taking.
   c. both of the above
   d. none of the above

_____ 4. Unlike the Piagetian approach, the psychometric approach concentrates on
   a. exploring *why* children give particular answers.
   b. tracing the ways that thought changes as children age.
   c. interview techniques.
   d. none of the above

_____ 5. Select the pair of psychometric theorists with the most nearly opposite views on the nature of intelligence.
   a. Spearman and Thurstone
   b. Binet and Simon
   c. Thurstone and Piaget
   d. Cattell and Horn

_____ 6. The intelligence quotient improved upon mental age, because it
   a. facilitated comparison of children of the same age.
   b. facilitated comparison of children of different ages.
   c. varied with age.
   d. was more accurate.

_____ 7. Which of the following has the IQ score been shown to predict with moderate accuracy?
   a. scholastic success
   b. occupational success
   c. a and b
   d. everyday adult functioning

_____ 8. Which of the following explanations of the relationship between IQ and socioeconomic status has been *rejected* by most investigators?
   a. Persons from different socioeconomic groups may have different levels of motivation to succeed on tests.

b. The tests themselves are biased toward concepts more familiar to white, middle-class students.

c. The relationship may be caused by environmental factors.

d. The relationship is traceable to differences in the ethnic composition of the lower and middle classes.

_____ 9. Which of the following factors is *not* associated with the lack of compensatory education at the high school level?

a. the failure of Feuerstein's widely implemented program to demonstrate improvements in IQ in this group

b. the widespread belief that adolescence is too late to overcome educational handicaps

c. the concentration of compensatory efforts on younger children

d. the tradition of concentrating resources on the most capable rather than the least capable of the economically disadvantaged

_____ 10. Studies indicate that schools that succeed in improving behavior and attendance

a. maintain a vocational emphasis.

b. do not support such frills as phones for students and hot drink machines.

c. emphasize individual instruction.

d. encourage parent involvement.

Answers to Self-Check Questions

1. c	**6.** b
2. a	**7.** c
3. b	**8.** d
4. d	**9.** a
5. a	**10.** d

CHAPTER 15

SOCIAL AND EMOTIONAL DEVELOPMENT DURING ADOLESCENCE

STUDY GOALS

After reading and studying Chaper 15, you should be able to:

1. Discuss both Erikson's and Marcia's theoretical work, which attempts to describe the adolescent's quest for personal identity.

2. Identify the societal factors which are influential in the adolescent's establishing an identity and deciding on an adult role.

3. Discuss the factors which have led to the current high rate of youth unemployment and the implications this has for an adolescent's future identity and values.

4. Describe the changes that have occurred in adolescent sexual behavior and use of alcohol and drugs in the past twenty years.

5. Discuss the developmental importance of friends during adolescence and the normative changes that occur in peer relations.

6. Describe the developmental changes that occur in regard to cliques, popularity, and conformity within the peer group.

7. Appreciate that the family is an important component in the adolescent's transition from childhood to adulthood.

8. Identify the developmental changes and adjustments that occur for both parents and adolescents in relation to family interactions and dynamics.

9. Describe Baumrind's work on parenting styles and the effects each style has on the adolescent's development and behavior.

10. Discuss the societal and parent-child factors which lead to adolescent abuse, and runaway, homeless, and delinquent behavior.

11. Discuss the importance of the work of the National Commission on Youth and the recommendations that the Commission has made to facilitate the transition from adolescence to a productive adult life.

REVIEWING THE CHAPTER

I. What are the developmental tasks of adolescence?
    (pp. 643–657; study goals 1–4)

In the midst of the many changes in the adolescent's physical, intellectual, and emotional development, the primary task is to establish a personal identity in terms of who she is and what she will become. This task of having to make decisions about their existence and future is all the more difficult because adolescents are in a transitional phase in their lives. The adolescent finds herself vacillating between the need for independence and the desire for dependence. Erik Erikson identifies this period as a quest for personal identity in which the psychosocial crisis is one of identity versus role confusion. The individual's identity is influenced by past experiences yet is more than a sum of successive identifications because the adolescent is capable of abstract thinking. Thus, as the adolescent thinks about ideology, life style and vocation, she develops a sense of continuity of the self. Erikson emphasizes that the task of identity formation is not easy and affects the way the individual deals with later periods in her development. Role confusion or identity diffusion can occur if the adolescent remains undecided about commitments or prematurely forms her identity.

The social context in which the adolescent lives influences identity formation. In complex societies where there are competing choices and values, identity formation is not an easy task. The adolescent has to make choices in light of her own talents, capacities, and the family's economic resources. The adolescent spends a great deal of time thinking about what she would like to do when she grows up and what she is capable of.

Youth unemployment, especially among under-educated and minority groups, is a national problem. With the decrease in unskilled jobs, these youth are faced with the prospects of being unemployed in adulthood. Education and job-training programs have proven to be successful and cost effective in preparing youth for the world of work. Given the shifts in labor market trends, many teens and young adults are making career choices not on the basis of aptitude or interests, but on the basis of available job openings. It has been found that the kinds of choices adolescents make and the values they adopt differ in times of war, peace, social unrest, and economic depression. For instance, adults who lived through the depression as children, appear to be very family centered, emphasize the responsibilities of parenthood, and the dependability of children.

The changes in sex roles and sexual behavior influence identity formation in adolescence. Although the changes in sex roles have had the greatest impact on girls, both adolescent girls and boys realize they have equal opportunities to assume any role in life they wish. One unfortunate outcome of the sexual revolution has been in the increase in adolescent motherhood. The poor health and poverty that often accompany teenage parenthood often have a devastating impact on educational and vocational goals.

II. How important are friends to the adolescent?
   (pp. 657–663; study goals 4–6)

The choice of friends is one of the major factors in the search for identity, as friends help determine one's life style and values and provide emotional support as the adolescent disengages from the family and establishes an independent life. Friends serve different functions as the adolescent develops. The emphasis changes from one of shared activities in early adolescence, to feeling secure in middle adolescence, to being more relaxed about individual differences among friends in late adolescence. Routinely, boys are about 2 years behind girls in reaching physiological and emotional maturity. Boys' timetable for friendships also vary from girls', however friendships are equally important for boys as for girls. During adolescence, teens enjoy spending time with a particular group of friends or cliques. The nature of these cliques changes from small, homogeneous, single-sex groups in early adolescence to larger groups with both sexes in late adolescence. Popularity with peers seems to be most affected by personality factors such as cheerfulness, friendliness, and enthusiasm. A teen who has no friends has been associated with low self-esteem and feeling different from the rest of the crowd. Recent evidence points to the fact that the need to conform and susceptibility to peer pressure decreases as the adolescent becomes older and more secure in her identity.

III. Is there a generation gap between adolescents and their parents?
   (pp. 663–676; study goals 7–11)

Although there is a shift in time spent with parents, research indicates that most adolescents are understanding of their parents and are understood by their parents. While teens talk to friends about social issues, they continue to use their parents to help make decisions about future educational and career goals. However, in their attempts to establish their own identity, they question their parents' ideology. The adolescent is in the process of adjusting to the physical, intellectual, and emotional changes that are occurring in her. At the same time the parents are learning to make adjustments in living with an adolescent. This demands establishing new patterns of authority and interaction. The task of parents is to guide the adolescent and offer her the support and advice she needs, and at the same time nurture her quest for independence.

As with younger children, parenting styles have important effects on the adolescent's development. Baumrind's work indicates that parents who have an authoritative style tend to have adolescents who are socially active, have high self-esteem, and can commit themselves to certain values and goals. Teens of authoritarian parents often have problems developing their own identity and withdraw from making commitments and evaluating life choices. The adolescents of permissive parents often feel rejected and confused from the lack of parental direction.

Recent studies reveal that physical and emotional maltreatment of adolescents is prevalent and related to inappropriate parenting styles and conflict between parents and teens. Since adolescents are able to physically strike back, psychological rather than physical abuse is more prevalent. Often those teens who are subjected to abuse or neglect run away from home, find themselves homeless, or adopt a life of violence and crime. The typical runaway episode is a spontaneous act which stems from conflict or frustration in the parent-teen relationship and reflects the adolescent's feelings of assumed parental rejection and anger at the parents' unwillingness to relax restrictions. Whereas runaways often return home, homeless youth are rejected by their families and often they are asked to leave. The families typically have financial problems and are characterized by divorce, abuse, and parental low self-esteem. Delinquent youths often come from runaway or homeless situations. Recently psychologists have found out that delinquent youths are likely to have low self-esteem, been subjected to abuse, and have a history of family and school problems. The National Commission on Youth has made numerous recommendations to alleviate some of the problems of adolescence. They have included changes in educational, employment and juvenile justice laws, which emphasize connections among the institutions that serve adolescents.

SIGNIFICANT CONCEPTS, TERMS, AND TOPICS

You should become familiar with and be able to explain the following concepts, terms, and topics. Most of the terms are highlighted in the margins of the text and some are also defined in the glossary at the end of the text.

identity vs. role confusion	*identity diffusion*
foreclosure	*moratorium*
social context	*vocational identity*
youth unemployment	*shared activities*
security	*individuality*
cliques	*crowd*
popularity	*rejection*
conformity	*authoritative parents*
authoritarian parents	*permissive parents*
runaway youth	*homeless youth*
delinquent youth	**National Commission on Youth**

SELF-CHECK

Choose the response that best answers the question or completes the statement.

_____ 1. A group of adolescents are standing outside school discussing one of their friends. In describing their friend, which of the following qualities would an adolescent rather than a child be more likely to use?
   a. school performance
   b. overt behavior
   c. physical appearance
   d. personality traits

_____ 2. The most popular substance which adolescents abuse is
   a. pills
   b. alcohol
   c. marijuana
   d. crack

_____ 3. Research indicates that an adolescent who uses marijuana usually goes on to use other drugs such as heroin or pills.
   a. true
   b. false

_____ 4. Adolescents of _____ parents have difficulty in developing their identity and often withdraw from making life choices.
   a. authoritarian
   b. indifferent
   c. authoritative
   d. permissive

_____ 5. The friendships boys have during adolescence tend to be _____ important than the friendships girls maintain.
   a. less
   b. more
   c. neither a nor b; friendships are equally important for boys and girls during adolescence.

_____ 6. Surveys of adolescent sexual behavior indicate that by age 18, _____ percent of teenage girls and _____ percent of teenage boys admit to being sexually active.
   a. 90; 90
   b. 60; 80
   c. 40; 50
   d. 70; 80

_____ 7. Adolescents who fail to develop a stable and clear sense of identity by the time they have reached their early twenties have, according to Erikson a prevailing sense of _____ .
   a. role moratorium
   b. role ambiguity
   c. role confusion
   d. role diffusion

_____ 8. In comparing the youth of the 1970s and the 1980s, the youth of the 1980s
a. are more depressed about the future.
b. are seeking to change the world.
c. are adhering to more traditional values.
d. all of the above
_____ 9. A sense of inner assurance and knowing where one is going are central to what Erikson calls
a. identity.
b. productivity.
c. intimacy.
d. role confusion.
_____ 10. Since the 1960s, surveys of adolescents and their parents indicate that there is not a generation gap between teens and their parents.
a. true
b. false

Answers to Self-Check Questions

1. d	**6.** d
2. b	**7.** c
3. a	**8.** c
4. a	**9.** a
5. c	**10.** a

ATYPICAL DEVELOPMENT IN ADOLESCENCE

STUDY GOALS

After reading and studying the section on Atypical Development in Adolescence, you should be able to:

1. List the symptoms of schizophrenia.

2. Describe the course of schizophrenia (i.e., indicate when it usually appears, whether its onset tends to be gradual or sudden, and the likelihood of recovery or remission).

3. Discuss the role of hereditary and environmental factors in the display of schizophrenic behavior.

4. Describe the biological differences found between schizophrenics and normal individuals.

5. Summarize the childhood characteristics of adolescents diagnosed as schizophrenic.

6. Discuss the advantages, disadvantages, and most effective use of antipsychotic drugs.

7. Name at least two reasons that it is often difficult to diagnose schizophrenia.

REVIEWING THE SECTION

Schizophrenia does not emerge until adolescence or the early adult years, but it is a serious psychiatric disorder characterized by extreme loss of contact with reality, marked deterioration of ability to function, hallucinations, bizarre behavior, disordered thought processes, deep apathy, and delusions of persecution or grandeur. Schizophrenics may also display senseless, illogical, and disconnected speech or abnormal affect, showing inappropriate emotional responses or failing to display any emotion at all. The various types of schizophrenia are diagnosed on the basis of which symptoms predominate. Contrary to popular belief, split personality is a psychiatric illness distinct from schizophrenia.

Even though the schizophrenic may experience brief periods of relief from his symptoms and may be aware of his own bizarre behavior, most of the time, his conduct causes him to become increasingly distant and remote to outsiders. He retreats into the self, becoming socially isolated and suspicious of others.

Schizophrenia is difficult to diagnose for several reasons. For instance, the psychotic behavior associated with schizophrenia can also occur in adolescents who abuse hallucinogens. Moreover, its onset usually occurs gradually, through a progressive deterioration in behavior between the ages of 15 and 24.

Research is currently underway to identify the characteristics of children most likely to be diagnosed as schizophrenic in adolescence. As yet, it is too early to draw conclusions from these inquiries, but it appears that schizophrenic adolescents are more likely to have been reclusive, aggressive, and antisocial children than adolescents not diagnosed as schizophrenic. However, some researchers have noted sex differences in the childhood characteristics of schizophrenic adolescents. Female schizophrenics are described as emotionally immature and passive during childhood, while their male counterparts are seen as irritable, aggressive, and defiant children.

Today, there is strong evidence that the *tendency* to become schizophrenic is inherited. However, non-genetic factors must also affect the display of schizophrenic symptoms, since even identical twins of schizophrenics often do not display the disorder. One indication of a genetic link is the fact that schizophrenia appears in only 1% of the general population, but occurs in 12% of children with one schizophrenic parent and 35 to 44% of children with two schizophrenic parents.

Several biological differences between schizophrenics and normal individuals have also been identified. These include differences in brain chemistry, especially in the handling of dopamine, which is present in excessive amounts in schizophrenics. Schizophrenics may also exhibit enlarged cavities in the interior of the brain, unusual patterns of electrical pulses, and decreased cerebral blood flow. Precisely *how* these biological differences act to produce schizophrenia is still not understood.

There is as yet no cure for schizophrenia. However, antipsychotic drugs first developed in the 1950s can decrease the rate of some of the bizarre behaviors associated with the disorder and make these patients more amenable to other treatments. Nonetheless, even these drugs are not effective with all schizophrenics and may be refused by many patients because they can cause serious side effects. Drug treatment should be used in combination with an effective treatment approach, such as a residential program that provides help in managing everyday problems and training in basic social skills. Other effective approaches focus on the families of schizophrenics, who may need support and help in understanding the symptoms, nature, and course of the disease.

Currently, the outlook for schizophrenics is much more hopeful than at the turn of the century. Those who experience a sudden rather than a gradual onset of the disease, who have a history of good social adjustment, and who experienced an emotional shock or an illness just prior to the onset of symptoms may suddenly overcome the disorder and suffer no relapses. Those who remain mentally ill are likely to be treated on an outpatient basis rather than to remain hospitalized for long periods. In addition, they may be helped to function in relatively normal circumstances and are much more likely to benefit from treatment than in the past.

SIGNIFICANT CONCEPTS, TERMS, AND TOPICS

You should become familiar with and be able to explain the following concepts, terms, and topics. Most of the terms are highlighted in the margins of the text and some are also defined in the glossary at the end of the text.

schizophrenia	*delusions*
delusions of grandeur	*delusions of persecution*
hallucinations	*abnormal affect*
dopamine	*split personality*
antipsychotic drugs	**dementia praecox**

SELF-CHECK

Choose the response that best answers the question or completes the statement.

_____ 1. Schizophrenics' hallucinations are
   a. typically auditory.
   b. typically visual.
   c. typically auditory *and* visual.
   d. usually multisensory experiences.

_____ 2. Schizophrenia is most widely attributed to
   a. familial dysfunction.
   b. genetic and biological vulnerability.
   c. genetic factors uninfluenced by the environment.
   d. none of the above

_____ 3. Treatment with antipsychotic drugs
   a. has proven to be useless with schizophrenics.
   b. should only be one aspect of an overall treatment program.
   c. prevents schizophrenic symptoms from recurring.
   d. causes no serious side effects.

_____ 4. Schizophrenia is difficult to diagnose because
   a. the onset of the disorder is usually sudden.
   b. the psychotic behavior associated with schizophrenia also occurs among youths who abuse hallucinogens.
   c. the disease only becomes noticeable in the late 20s.
   d. none of the above

_____ 5. Which of the following is *not* a symptom of schizophrenia?
   a. inability to tolerate being alone
   b. hallucinations
   c. abnormal affect
   d. incoherent or disconnected speech

_____ 6. Biological differences between schizophrenics and normal people include all of the following *except*
   a. decreased regional cerebral blood flow.
   b. presence of excessive amounts of dopamine in the brain.
   c. anatomical abnormalities in the limbic system.
   d. unusual patterns of cerebral electrical impulses.

_____ 7. Which is the most accurate statement about the relationship between schizophrenia and genetic and environmental factors?
   a. Schizophrenia appears to be a wholly genetic disorder with a Mendelian pattern of inheritance.
   b. Schizophrenia appears to be caused most often by such environmental factors as familial dysfunction.
   c. Since the identical twin of a schizophrenic may not exhibit the disorder, some environmental component may be important.
   d. Schizophrenia is usually traceable to prenatal or perinatal brain injury; neither genetic nor subsequent environmental influences are significant.

Answers to Self-Check Questions

1. a	**5.** a
2. b	**6.** c
3. b	**7.** c
4. b	

CONCLUSION

CHILD DEVELOPMENT AND THE LIFE CYCLE

STUDY GOALS

After reading and studying the Conclusion, you should be able to:

1. Appreciate that developmental psychology is concerned with the sequential progression and change in behavior that occurs at any age in the human life cycle.

2. Discuss the contributions of gender, health, ethnic group, experiences, events, and social class in the study of the adult development.

3. Compare and contrast Erikson's and Levinson's stages of adult development and the issues they represent.

4. Describe the myths and recent research associated with midlife crisis and old age.

5. Discuss the demographic changes that are occurring within the United States population and the implications for programs and policy for children, families, and the elderly.

6. Describe the work of Kubler-Ross and the hospice movement as a means of allowing individuals to approach death and dying in a respectful manner.

7. Appreciate that the study of children includes the study of adults for both interact in the context of social reality.

REVIEWING THE CHAPTER

I.   What do we know about adult development?
     (pp. 686–692; study goals 1 and 2)

     The study of adulthood and aging and the perception of its relevance to the field of developmental psychology are recent. It is now recognized that throughout the lifespan people not only experience the physiological changes associated with increasing age, they also undergo many changes as the result of events and problems they experience. They change in their perceptions and expectations of themselves and others and in their relationships with others. Research on adulthood has dispelled some of our myths about adult development such as that senility is a normal aging process and that there is a universal decline in intelligence. Just as developmental milestones are important in understanding children, so are they in gaining an understanding of adulthood. For instance, getting married, becoming a parent or grandparent, and retiring trigger changes within the individual. However, these events are not universally experienced nor do they happen at the same time for all individuals. Thus, much of what happens during adulthood can be described as culturally conditioned in which a chronological framework is inappropriate. Neugarten, (1968) coined the expression *social clock* to explain many of the milestones that mark an individual's passage through the life cycle. She states that every culture has a sense of social timing for appropriate social behaviors such as career, marriage, or children. The social clock varies from culture to culture, varies within cultures, and changes with time.

II. What are the current theories of life span development?
     (pp. 692–701; study goals 3 and 4)

The most widely respected theory of life span development is Erikson's (1963) description of psychosocial development that occurs in 8 stages or crises from birth through old age. The 3 stages that occur during the adult years are: intimacy versus isolation; generativity versus stagnation; and integrity versus despair. These stages are built upon the earlier stages of childhood and they represent some of the central issues that are faced by individuals during their adult years. Intimacy versus isolation occurs during early adulthood and is characterized by the individual's need to establish intimate relations with others and acquire from these an awareness of the value of love. The longest stage, generativity versus stagnation, encompasses the years between early adulthood and old age. This stage is characterized by the individual's sense of productivity and the need to create something that will outlive him. The final stage, integrity versus despair, occurs late in life as individuals evaluate their life accomplishments and experiences and hopefully arrive at the conclusion that life has been meaningful and productive.

More recently research by Levinson indicated that individuals experience not only broad stages but also periods of transition in their adult lives. In studying a group of working and middle-class men, he proposes that there are 5 eras within the lifespan that include a series of developmental periods and transitions. During the stable periods, individuals build a life structure by making choices and striving to accomplish certain goals. During the transitions, they reappraise previous choices and goals and often terminate their existing life structure and initiate a new one. During early adulthood individuals begin to forge an identity and the life structure of an adult. They also go through the age 30 transition in which they reevaluate choices they have made and life becomes more serious. A similar pattern emerges in middle adulthood with the transition of the midlife crisis. Recent work indicates that middle age is associated with a great deal of stress and that there are also individual differences in the extent to which a midlife crisis is experienced. The current work is attempting to clarify what is myth and what is experienced by both men and women within our culture.

III. What is the relationship between children and adults over the life span? (pp. 702–712; study goals 5–7)

Children and adults constantly interact in the context of social reality. Their relationships change over the life span. There are adjustments to be made in how parents care for and interact with their children and in how the parents interact with each other. It has been noted that parents often experience what has been labeled the empty nest syndrome. Recent research indicates that today most mothers do not experience a sense of depression when their children leave home; they feel good about themselves and their children. Rather, it appears that fathers often become depressed. During middle age, adults also face the responsibilities of caring for aged parents at the same time as they are facing the increased financial responsibilities associated with the growth of their children.

Old age is also a dynamic period in which the individual has to adapt to such events as retirement, grandparenthood, and widowhood. Recent work dispels the negative stereotypes of old age and is beginning to give way to a more realistic view that the elderly do not necessarily share a common set of circumstances and that old age in and of itself is not necessarily debilitating. Recent work indicates that social scientists know very little about the diverse nature of the role of the grandparent in our society. We do know that becoming a grandparent provides a sense of biological continuity and that there is often a special relationship between grandparents and grandchildren.

The study of how people approach the end of their life has been investigated extensively by Kubler-Ross. In studying 200 patients who were dying, she found that they seem to experience 5 stages (denial, anger, depression, bargaining, and acceptance) in confronting their impending death. The use of hospices has made the prospect of death easier for both the family and the dying person.

In conclusion, it is important to remember that throughout the cycle of human life there is a potential for growth and development. As a society that recognizes the changing needs of children and adults, it is vital to recognize that at certain points in time individuals may need support and intervention to enhance the quality of their lives.

SIGNIFICANT CONCEPTS, PEOPLE, AND TOPICS

You should become familiar with and be able to explain the following concepts, people, and topics. Most of the terms are highlighted in the margins of the text and some are also defined in the glossary at the end of the text.

social clock	*intimacy vs. isolation*
generativity vs. stagnation	*integrity vs. despair*
midlife crisis	*empty nest syndrome*
denial	*anger*
bargaining	*hospice*
Erik Erikson	*Daniel Levinson*
Bernice Neugarten	*Elisabeth Kubler-Ross*

SELF-CHECK

Choose the response that best answers the question or completes the statement.

_____ 1. Bower argues that the changes adults experience after age 20 are largely
   a. cultural.
   b. biological.
   c. age-related.
   d. all of the above

_____ 2. Research on adult intellectual performance indicates that intelligence
   a. universally declines with age.
   b. may show some decline in certain abilities with age, but at the same time there are improvements in areas of mental functioning.
   c. plateaus in the early 20s and stays the same for quite awhile.
   d. none of the above

_____ 3. A chronological framework to the study of adulthood has been found to be
   a. inappropriate
   b. appropriate

_____ 4. Identify which reference to Neugarten's social clock phenomenon is not true.
   a. It varies within cultures.
   b. It varies from culture to culture.
   c. It is universal.
   d. It changes with time.
   e. None, they are all true.

_____ 5. Middle-aged people
   a. become more concerned with relating to young people.
   b. seem to lose perspective on their place in the life cycle.
   c. seem to be in a stable, stress-free period of their life.
   d. engage in personal and vocational reassessment.

_____ 6. The study of adult development
   a. is separate and distinct from issues in developmental psychology.
   b. provides the opportunity to think about the growth and development of children in the context of their social reality.
   c. allows us to better understand how culture and social clocks influence behavior and development.
   d. b & c
   e. a, b, & c

Answers to Self-Check Questions

1. a	**4.** c
2. b	**5.** d
3. a	**6.** d

1 2 3 4 5 6 7 8 9